Endorsements

In *Beyond Poverty*, Terry Dalrymple presents the challenge of moving Christian servants of God beyond sustainable development work in a single village to transformational movements that sweep the countryside, based on the strategy of Community Health Evangelism (CHE), a global network which Terry founded and now serves as coordinator. I have come to know and appreciate Terry as a co-catalyst for Transform World's Poverty Challenge, which focuses on transforming communities among the unreached and unengaged people who live in the 10/40 Window. Terry envisions the Million Village Challenge—which is strategically based on clusters, models, and tipping points—as a bold mission initiative that has the goal of reaching one million mission villages where the remaining unreached people groups and the poorest of the poor live.

Luis Bush, PhD
Former International Director, AD 2000 & Beyond
International Facilitator, Transform World 2020

I am so honored to endorse Terry Dalrymple's book. Terry introduced me to wholistic mission work years ago and mentored me through the transition from an evangelistic relief model of our church to a wholistic evangelism model. I cannot even begin to tell you the transformational impact his teaching has had on our global missions work and our church. And now it's documented in his book. This book captures a lifetime of one man's obedience to God as he presents what he has learned. *Beyond Poverty* is a playbook for those of us who desire to restore dignity and honor to those who are struggling and giving them hope. Truly a masterpiece!

Larrie Fraley
Founding member and Lead Global Outreach Pastor, Christ's Church of the Valley, Peoria, Arizona

Even among the mass of global volunteerism in our world today, there is still a need for leaders—even more so, generals. They must see beyond the obvious, into the seemingly unknown realms, lay hold of vision, and cast then that vision to the masses in order for great things to be moved from the realms of impossibilities to the daily realities of changed lives. My friend, my colaborer and mentor, Terry Dalrymple, is such a general. For decades, and in this soul-challenging book, with its scriptural principles and proven practices, he seeks to inspire and call to arms every true believer in Christ to engage wholeheartedly in obeying the singular mission commandment to "make disciples," while alleviating wholistic poverty for untold numbers of the world's poor. Be ready to learn and to join the movement of transformation that is already shaking the globe!

Rev. Keith Holloway
Senior Director, Missions Development

In *Beyond Poverty*, Terry has beautifully laid out the Biblical basis for wholistic ministry and foundational principles for transformational movements. The inspiring stories of movements that he shares have been catalyzed by ordinary people with an extraordinary passion to be obedient to the cause of Christ. The book is easy to read, very informational, and hopefully the reader will be inspired to become a part of this movement that will ultimately bring new life to a million villages.

Dr. Ravi I. Jayakaran
President/CEO, Medical Ambassadors International
Catalyst of Integral Mission, The Lausanne Movement

Beyond Poverty could well be one of the most influential books for this century, as it is a catalytic spark for global awareness of the gathering wave to fulfill the Great Commission of our Lord. The Joshua Project clearly stated several years ago that the remaining unreached tribes are poor and rural. May God open your mind, eyes, and heart through this amazing work!

Hal Jones
Founder and former President, Global Hope Network International
Founder, Geneva Institute for Leadership and Public Policy (GILPP)

Beyond Poverty gives a blueprint for a true integral missional approach that leads to sustainable community—and church owned development. Terry Dalrymple convincingly demonstrates through practical examples that this outcome is the result of an unconditional commitment to follow Jesus and to seamlessly integrate evangelism and compassion with an intentional focus on working collaboratively within the body of Christ. This book can become a new standard reference for Christian professionals in the global development arena. Terry's deep experience as practitioner and master trainer in gospel-driven community development enriches the work throughout. This is a must-read for anyone with a serious interest in the growing role of development in the changing missiological landscape.

Gil H. Odendaal, PhD
Former Senior Vice President, Integral Mission World Relief

BEYOND POVERTY

Beyond Poverty: Multiplying Christ-Centered Community Development
© 2021 by Terry Dalrymple. All rights reserved.

No part of this book may be reproduced, stored in a retrieval system, or transmitted in any form or by any means—electronic, mechanical, photocopy, recording, or otherwise—without prior written permission from the publisher, except brief quotations used in connection with reviews. This manuscript may not be entered into AI, even for AI training. For permission, email permissions@wclbooks.com. For corrections, email editor@wclbooks.com.

William Carey Publishing (WCP) publishes resources to shape and advance the missiological conversation in the world. We publish a broad range of thought-provoking books and do not necessarily endorse all opinions set forth here or in works referenced within this book.

The URLs included in this workbook are provided for personal use only and are current as of the date of publication, but the publisher disclaims any obligation to update them after publication.

All Scripture quotations, unless otherwise indicated, are taken from the Holy Bible, New International Version®, NIV®. Copyright ©1984 by Biblica, Inc.™ Scripture quotations marked "2011 NIV" are taken from THE HOLY BIBLE, NEW INTERNATIONAL VERSION®, NIV® Copyright © 1973, 1978, 1984, 2011 by Biblica, Inc.® Used by permission. All rights reserved worldwide.

Scripture quotations marked "NRSV" are taken from the New Revised Standard Version Bible, copyright © 1989 National Council of the Churches of Christ in the United States of America. Used by permission. All rights reserved worldwide.

Published by William Carey Publishing
10 W. Dry Creek Cir
Littleton, CO 80120 | www.missionbooks.org

William Carey Publishing is a ministry of Frontier Ventures
Pasadena, CA | www.frontierventures.org

Cover and Interior Designer: Mike Riester
Copyeditor: Andy Sloan
Managing Editor: Melissa Hicks

ISBNs: 978-1-64508-317-7 (paperback)
       978-1-64508-320-7 (epub)

Printed Worldwide

28 27 26 25 24   2 3 4 5 6   IN

Library of Congress Control Number: 2022946758

BEYOND POVERTY

Multiplying Christ-Centered Community Development

Terry Dalrymple

Available at missionbooks.org

Contents

Preface	ix
Introduction	xi
Chapter 1: Answering the Call	1
Chapter 2: Accelerating Change for the Poor	9
Chapter 3: Change Begins Here	13
Chapter 4: Changing Together	23
Chapter 5: Change That God Intends	41
Chapter 6: Change That Multiplies	57
Chapter 7: Change That Informs and Inspires— Stories of Transformation	87
Chapter 8: Models, Clusters, and Tipping Points	119
Chapter 9: Be Part of the Change	123
Appendix A: What Others Are Saying about CHE	132
Appendix B: A Brief History of Community Health Evangelism	133
Bibliography	138
About the Author	140

Preface

As a manager of international Christian development programs and then as consultant to Christian development ministries globally, I have had the privilege of getting a look "under the hood" at the engine that makes transformational development happen. I have witnessed projects in a single village fail. I have also seen work in single villages catalyze transformational movements that lifted one community after another out of cycles of poverty while multiplying disciples in every place.

These experiences have left a burden in my heart to share what I have learned with everyone investing in poor villages. It must be the same feeling experienced by conscientious investment counselors who want to see their clients' investments bring a maximum return.

I have seen gospel transformation move from community to community in many places around the world, changing the lives of the village poor forever. I am convinced from experience and research that we don't have to be content with doing projects that improve the situation for a small group of people, but rather that with the same level of investment we can catalyze transformational movements that will sweep the countryside. In this book, I will articulate proven principles for facilitating change in individuals and communities and then multiplying that change from village to village.

As I often do when I begin to speak at various venues, I will begin here by asking this question: "Can you claim that the development work you are doing has the potential to transform nations?" If you cannot, then this book is for you.

I am writing in the midst of the global COVID-19 pandemic. The United Nations predicted early on in this crisis that the number of people dying from starvation could double during the pandemic.[1] David Beasley, executive director of the United Nations World Food Program, pled with the U.N. Security Council to take action, asserting that the coronavirus pandemic threatened to detonate an unprecedented global humanitarian catastrophe, pushing millions to the brink of starvation.[2]

As I write, these warnings are turning into realities. I am reading now of the horrors. We are seeing a great reversal in our progress in the fight against poverty. The number of people living on less than $1.90 a day had been dropping steadily since 2008. With COVID-19, those numbers are rising—and fast. An article in the May 23, 2020, edition of *The Economist* refers to this as "the great reversal."[3]

---

1 "U.N. Warns Number of People Starving to Death Could Double amid Pandemic," NPR, May 5, 2020, https://www.npr.org/sections/coronavirus-live-updates/2020/05/05/850470436/u-n-warns-number-of-people-starving-to-death-could-double-amid-pandemic.

2 Covid-19 Could Detonate a 'hunger pandemic.' With Millions at Risk, the World Must Act." *The Washington Post*, April 22, 2020, https://www.washingtonpost.com/opinions/2020/04/22/covid-19-could-detonate-hunger-pandemic-with-millions-risk-world-must-act/.

3 "The Great Reversal: Covid-19 Is Undoing Years of Progress in Curbing Global Poverty," *The Economist*,

Migrant workers in cities all over the developing world have lost their jobs and the ability to support their families in rural areas. Villagers and whole villages that looked to their relatives in the city for help when a harvest failed can no longer do so.[4] Migrant workers in India were laid off at the same time transportation was cut off to their villages. At least twenty-two migrants in New Delhi died trying to get home after a lockdown, as thousands of migrants tried to walk back to their villages.[5]

Villagers like those from South Sudan who have fled from war and settled in refugee camps in Uganda are at risk of starvation. The World Food Program has recently reported that they have been forced to cut funding to refugees in Uganda by 30 percent, and that funds continue to dry up. I am beginning to hear reports from our partners in the field.

A few weeks ago, I received an appeal from a member of our network living and working among refugees in a camp in Uganda. He pleaded for help, sharing that rations had been reduced significantly and that the majority of the families he served were fighting starvation. Suicides were on the rise. Young people were resorting to stealing and violence in their fight to survive. Marriages were breaking up, as men failed to meet the needs of their wives and children. Orphans and widows were being hurt the worst. He wished they could grow food to supply what would be lacking in the future, but admitted that they didn't have seed or tools. In addition to this personal plea, I read an article just yesterday that told the story of a Sudanese man in a refugee camp who sold his children in order to survive.

I have had to wrestle with feelings of anger when presented with these facts. Compassion would have been a more appropriate response, but it felt to me that little thought was being given to the plight of poor villagers as strategies were rolled out to deal with the crisis in the cities. The last paragraph in the article from *The Economist* cited instances where global crises created solidarity with the poor, concluding with these words: "It would be wonderful if Covid-19 could inspire similar efforts. But for now, the rich world is too distracted by its own problems to pay much heed to the poor."[6]

We will not pay heed to the poor we have not heard anything about. This book is your opportunity to hear the cry of the poor, enter into their struggle, and learn to facilitate gospel-based transformational movements that will alleviate poverty while multiplying disciples of Christ among the poorest of the poor.

May 23, 2020, https://www.economist.com/international/2020/05/23/covid-19-is-undoing-years-of-progress-in-curbing-global-poverty.

4 Ibid.

5 "Covid-19: At Least 22 Migrants Die While Trying to Get Home During Lockdown," *Scroll*, March 29, 2020, https://scroll.in/latest/957570/covid-19-lockdown-man-collapses-dies-halfway-while-walking-home-300-km-away-from-delhi.

6 "The Great Reversal."

Introduction

A Cry from the Village

I was leaving a small village in the highlands of Northern Thailand with a team of national missionaries. We were standing in the middle of the red dirt road (pictured above), just wide enough for a single vehicle to navigate. The road cut through the green foliage of the tropical forest like a ribbon, connecting remote villages with the outside world. We couldn't have traveled this road, even in a four-wheel drive, at certain times of the year; but on this warm day in dry season, we managed to bump and squeeze our vehicle along until we arrived at what was home to about three hundred Hmong people.

The village was about the same size as Nazareth, the small community in which Jesus grew up about two thousand years ago. The people lived in what would appear to outsiders as temporary shelters, and which had no running water. We saw barefoot children in tattered clothes.

The Hmong are one of several impoverished ethnic minorities living in the highlands of Northern Thailand, Myanmar, Cambodia, and Laos. Because of extreme poverty, children from these areas have been particularly vulnerable to exploitation and are often victims of sex trafficking or forced labor.[7] Traffickers, often from the cities of Chiang Mai or Bangkok, promise parents they will get jobs for their daughters in the cities as waitresses or maids. These parents, looking for a better quality of life and a future for their offspring, sell their own children into slavery.

---
7 Friends of Thai Daughters website, 2018, https://www.friendsofthaidaughters.org/human-trafficking-crisis.

Having done well economically in recent years, the nation of Thailand is considered one of the great development success stories of the past three decades. However, this economic prosperity has not yet alleviated poverty for the poorest in the country, with over 80 percent of them living in rural communities like the village at the end of this road.[8]

The poor in Thai villages, trapped in cycles of poverty and disease, share the same concerns as others in rural poor communities all over the world—inadequate sanitation, unsafe drinking water, higher rates of infant and child mortality, low income, food insecurity, and limited access to educational opportunities.

The "village" is not only home to the world's poorest, but it is also home to many of those who are least reached with the gospel—frequently minorities who adhere to traditional beliefs or folk religions. The Hmong in the village at the end of this road believe that spirits control the quality of their lives. A medium in the village communicates with the spirits and informs the people of the spirits' desires. The people obey the instructions the medium gives them. I was told while I was there that the elders in a nearby village refused to allow the government to pipe clean water into their homes because they believed putting pipes in the ground would upset the spirits and bring harm to the people of their community.

I visited the village at the end of the road with a team of Christian development workers dedicated to bringing hope and change to this remote community. On our way out of the village, we passed what appeared to be handrails on either side of the road, creating an illusion that we were crossing a bridge. I turned to one of the team members, a Hmong believer, and asked what we were seeing.

"This is a spirit bridge," she explained. "Villagers offer sacrifices here and invite departed spirits to return to the village."

She went on, "If a person is seriously ill, it is because an essential life force (a spirit) has gone away down the road. To remedy this situation, the Hmong built this spirit bridge where they offer sacrifices in order to welcome the departed spirits back. When the spirits pass over the bridge and return, the sick person is made well."

As I stood at this spirit bridge and listened to my team member's explanation, I couldn't help but ask the question, "When will the Hmong invite the Spirit of Jesus to pass this way? His Spirit is the only life force that can bring real healing and restore wholeness to their lives and community."

---

8 "The World Bank in Thailand," World Bank website, September 2020, https://www.worldbank.org/en/country/thailand/overview.

Introduction   xiii

A Call to the Church

If we want to bring the gospel to the world's poorest, many still unreached with no Christian witness among them, then we must go to the rural poor village. That is where 85 percent of them live.[9]

While governments around the world are focused on poverty alleviation for people living in acute deprivation, the church is uniquely positioned to actually achieve the goal. The church may well be the only institution with the capacity to alleviate poverty among the world's poorest, and it is certainly the only institution with the capacity to change the trajectory of their lives for eternity.

The church is the largest army of volunteers in the world, and their King is calling. He is calling his followers to go to the poor, many with no gospel witness among them. He is sending his ambassadors to remote places in anticipation of the day when a great crowd gathers around his throne from every tribe, tongue, and nation.[10]

In 2017, in preparation for a speech to a group of lawmakers at the United Nations in Geneva, I learned of a new tool for measuring acute poverty being used by the United Nations Development Programme (UNDP), called the Multidimensional Poverty Index.[11] Initial research using this index indicated that there were approximately 1.6 billion people in our world living in acute poverty, [12] and that 1.3 billion of those were living in rural poor villages.[13]

In preparation for my presentation, I wanted to know how many villages those 1.3 billion people occupied. I searched the Internet for data on the size of the average rural village in the developing world. Although I was unsuccessful, I did find that the average village size in India was 1,300 people (1,299.96 to be exact).[14] Since more than one-third of the global village poor live in India,[15] I used 1,300 as the average village size for the sake of my calculation. When I took the total of 1.3 billion rural poor and divided it by an average village size of 1,300, my calculator returned an answer of one million.

---

9 "Global MPI 2018," Oxford Poverty & Human Development Initiative (OPHI), Oxford Department of International Development, https://ophi.org.uk/multidimensional-poverty-index/global-mpi-2018/.

10 Revelation 7:9–10.

11 "Global MPI 2018."

12 Transform World website, https://www.transform-world.net.

13 Sabina Alkire, Mihika Chatterjee, Adriana Conconi, Suman Seth, and Ana Vaz, "Poverty in Rural and Urban Areas: Direct Comparisons Using the Global MPI 2014," Oxford Poverty & Human Development Initiative (OPHI), Oxford Department of International Development, June 2014, https://opendocs.ids.ac.uk/opendocs/bitstream/handle/123456789/11802/Poverty-in-Rural.pdf?sequence=1&isAllowed=y.

14 Census of India website archives, May 14, 2007, https://web.archive.org/web/20070514045222/http://www.censusindia.gov.in/, retrieved April 9, 2012. (833.1 million people living in villages divided by 640,867 villages = 1299.957 average village size.)

15 "Global MPI 2018."

I looked in astonishment at that number and checked it again to make sure I hadn't made a mistake. I got the same answer—one million villages! I felt a surge of emotion as I gazed at my computer screen!

One million was a number that had been in my mind and on my lips for some time already. Several years earlier, I had been invited to serve with Transform World 2020 in a new initiative. Transform World 2020 is a global partnership of evangelicals calling the church worldwide to consider the critical challenges of our time.[16] Poverty was listed among the challenges. Hal Jones, my friend and colleague, invited me to serve with him as co-catalyst for this poverty challenge. Hal had already named the campaign we would champion together the "Million Village Challenge." For several years already, we had been calling and equipping the church to catalyze transformational movements that would eventually reach a million villages.

We have our number! If the church will answer the call to alleviate poverty and make followers of Jesus among the rural poor, then we are looking at a Million Village Challenge—the challenge to bring Christ's transformation to one million villages.

Call me a pie-in-the-sky visionary, but I believe the vision of catalyzing transformational movements in a million villages is achievable. We will need to think differently about how we serve the poor. We will need to move beyond development projects in single villages to transformational movements that sweep the countryside. We will need to collaborate and work together as one body. But it can be done!

When you finish reading this book, you will understand key principles and proven strategies for catalyzing movements that multiply disciples while lifting whole communities out of cycles of poverty and disease. The water tower graphic below illustrates these principles, which will be addressed in more detail in chapter 6. You will also know how to work in ways that empower individuals and communities for God-intended change, and to equip them to multiply that change from home to home and village to village. And you will know how to connect with others who share your passion for the poorest and least-reached and become part of the million-village movement.

---

16 Transform World website.

TRANSFORMATIONAL DEVELOPMENT
Lives and communities transformed by the love of Christ.

Water towers come in many shapes and sizes; however, they need strong legs and a solid foundation on which to stand. So it is with Transformational Development Programs.

LOCAL OWNERSHIP
- Give people with a vision what **they can do** to improve the quality of their lives and minister to others' needs.
- Involve people in identifying needs and resources, and making plans.
- Build cooperation; get people working together.
- Don't blueprint plans from the outside

MULTIPLICATION
- Focus on use of local resources.
- Avoid dependency on outsiders.
- Look beyond sustainability to multiplication.

INTEGRATION
- Keep faith and works together.
- Promote complete obedience to all Jesus commanded.
- Promote development in wisdom, stature, and favor with God and man.

DEVELOPMENT
- Involve people as responsible participants rather than passive recipients.
- Build capacity rather than create dependency.
- Help people to do for themselves rather than doing things for them.

- Cast VISION rather than blueprinting action plans.
- Pose PROBLEMS rather than solutions.
- DIALOGUE rather than lecture.

PARTICIPATORY LEARNING

TRUTH

CHAPTER 1

Answering the Call
Change in a Million Villages

Community Development as Mission Strategy

Christian community development has only recently become acceptable mission strategy in many evangelical circles. The reason for this is in our history. I say "our history" because I identify myself as an evangelical.

Evangelicals weathered a long battle with theological liberals at the end of the nineteenth century and the beginning of the twentieth. Liberalism attempted to reconcile the Christian faith with evolutionary thought, higher criticism, philosophical idealism, and world religion. As a consequence, liberals embraced a low view of Scripture, denying its authority as the inspired Word of God. Liberal theologians were also the primary advocates of what started out as "Social Christianity," or sometimes "Christian Socialism," but later became the more moderate "Social Gospel." The goal of the Social Gospel was justice for the urban poor through programs that would build the kingdom of God on earth.[17]

Against the onslaughts of liberalism, evangelicals upheld the Scriptures as the inerrant Word of God and defended the miracles and the atoning work of Christ. However, they emerged from the battle with a low view of social action. They rejected social justice as part of the primary mission of the church and focused almost exclusively on evangelism and church planting.

My wife, Jeannie, and I were appointed as church-planting missionaries to the Philippines in 1985. Shortly after our arrival on the field, a veteran pulled me aside with a single word of advice: "If you feed somebody today, they will be hungry again tomorrow. If you save their soul today, they will be saved forever."

His advice summarized the philosophy of ministry of my new colleagues and was consistent with what the majority of evangelicals at that time believed about the mission of the church. We had not been sent to the Philippines to care for people's physical needs, but to preach and plant churches. I had no idea at the time, but God was already at work calling evangelicals back to a biblical wholism that would bring evangelism and compassion back together. He would change me in the process.

---

17 "History of the Social Gospel," PBS.org, December 26, 2003, https://www.pbs.org/now/society/socialgospel.html.

The discussion among evangelicals began in 1974 when a committee headed by Rev. Billy Graham convened the first International Congress on World Evangelization. This consultation, held in Lausanne, Switzerland, drew more than 2,300 evangelical leaders from 150 countries. These men and women participated in plenary sessions and Bible studies, as well as discussions and debates over theology, strategy, and methods of evangelism. The gathering produced "The Lausanne Covenant," a declaration that was "intended to define the necessity, responsibilities, and goals of spreading the Gospel."[18] In the covenant is a section defining "The Nature of Evangelism" and a separate section addressing the question of "Christian Social Responsibility." The covenant left these two duties side by side without spelling out their relationship to each other, except to say that "in the church's mission of sacrificial service, evangelism is primary."

In 1982, the Lausanne Committee for World Evangelization and the World Evangelical Alliance sponsored the International Consultation on the Relationship between Evangelism and Social Responsibility, in Grand Rapids, Michigan. This follow-up to the Lausanne Congress was convened to further the discussion of the role of social action in the mission of the church and to define the relationship between social action and evangelism. The drafting committee, under the chairmanship of Rev. John Stott, published a report entitled "Evangelism and Social Responsibility."[19] Champions of wholistic mission, or the integration of evangelism and social action, emerged from this discussion. I will mention only a few who have influenced my thinking to one degree or another: Vinay K. Samuel (India), C. Rene Padilla (Argentina), John M. Perkins (United States), and John R. Stott (Great Britain).

Several books that were written between 1993 and 2009 have served to translate the integration of evangelism and social action into practical strategies for missionaries. In 1993, John Perkins wrote *Beyond Charity: A Call to Christian Community Development*. This book calls the church to action, bringing reconciliation and restoration to broken communities in the inner cities of North America. Perkins was one of the first to call for a serious, comprehensive, community development plan that enables the people to take responsibility for the improvement of their own neighborhoods. He believed the desperate problems in the inner city could not be solved without strong commitment and risky actions on the part of ordinary Christians with heroic faith.

Bryant Myers advanced the dialogue around Christian community development with a modern classic titled *Walking with the Poor* (World Vision

---

18 Lausanne I: The International Congress on World Evangelization, Lausanne, Switzerland, July 16–25, 1974, https://www.lausanne.org/gatherings/congress/lausanne-1974. The Lausanne Covenant is available at https://www.lausanne.org/content/covenant/lausanne-covenant.

19 "Evangelism and Social Responsibility: An Evangelical Commitment," Lausanne Occasional Paper 21, A Joint Publication of the Lausanne Committee for World Evangelization and the World Evangelical Fellowship, June 1982, https://www.lausanne.org/content/lop/lop-21.

International, 1999). Myers showed how Christian mission can contribute to dismantling poverty and social evil. He drew from many sources to lay out a biblical framework and principles for Christian community development that is integrated, sustainable, and transformative.

In 2009, Steve Corbett and Brian Fikkert published their work titled *When Helping Hurts*. They called on those serving the poor to understand the complexities of poverty and to employ strategies that do no harm, respect every person's dignity, and empower the materially poor. They championed the idea that sustainable change comes not from the outside in, but from the inside out.

In reviewing the books still on the market about Christian community development, the last word in the conversation seems to have been the articulation of principles and strategies for helping without hurting—empowering the materially poor for sustainable development rather than creating unhealthy dependencies. Building on principles popularized by *When Helping Hurts*, I want to move the discussion beyond questions of empowerment and sustainable development to offer strategies for accelerating poverty alleviation globally by catalyzing transformational movements. In this book I will offer proven principles, case studies, and a strategy for multiplying change from village to village and country to country.

The purpose of this book is to move beyond doing sustainable development in a single village to catalyzing transformational movements that sweep the countryside. My intent is not to tear down principles of sustainable development, but to reiterate and build on them.

> **The purpose of this book is to move beyond doing sustainable development in a single village to catalyzing transformational movements that sweep the countryside.**

Truly alleviating poverty and improving the quality of life for those we serve is satisfying, and it is rewarding to see the poor released from unhealthy dependencies and take their place as active participants in their own development processes. However, I believe there are still bigger opportunities in front of us—opportunities that have never before existed in all of history. Taking advantage of these opportunities will require that we refuse to be content with our present success and move the discussion beyond sustainability to multiplication.

In my work, I have seen the multiplication of deep and lasting change from village to village on a huge scale. Villagers who have transformed their own villages become champions of change, facilitating sustainable development processes in homes and communities around them. The result has been life-changing movements.

In the pages to follow, I will lay out the principles and practices that facilitated these transformative movements. Before we can do that, however, we need to understand the context in which we are working.

The Poverty Picture: Understanding the Complexities of Multidimensional Poverty

For years, extreme poverty has been defined by the World Bank in terms of income. The current global poverty line at the World Bank is people living on less than $1.90 per day.[20] New studies at Oxford, however, have demonstrated that poverty is multidimensional, and cannot be adequately defined by income alone. There are many reasons for this conclusion. Among them, income is not usually the medium of exchange in rural poor communities, where people live off the land and survive by trading goods and services. Using income as the sole measure of poverty fails to take into account the many pressures holding people down.

Here are some vivid illustrations of what those stresses might be: (1) Forty-two percent of the multi-dimensionally poor live in households where no adult has even five years of education; (2) Fifty-four percent live in households where at least one person is undernourished; (3) Forty-three percent live in households where at least one child has died; and (4) Eighty-one percent live in households where sanitation is inadequate.[21]

Researchers with the Oxford Poverty and Human Development Initiative (OPHI) have created a "Multidimensional Poverty Index" as a way of measuring the many factors that contribute to the deprivation of the poor. The original study identified three primary factors, or dimensions, of poverty: education, health, and standard of living. These dimensions are studied and measured using ten indicators.[22]

Three Dimensions of Poverty

Health	Nutrition
Health	Child mortality
Education	Years of schooling
Education	School attendance
Living Standards	Cooking fuel
Living Standards	Sanitation
Living Standards	Drinking water
Living Standards	Electricity
Living Standards	Housing
Living Standards	Assets

Source: Oxford University Global Multidimensional Poverty Index, 2018

---

20 "FAQs: Global Poverty Line Update," The World Bank, September 30, 2015, http://www.worldbank.org/en/topic/poverty/brief/global-poverty-line-faq.

21 Tom Murphy, "More Than 1.6 Billion People Live in Poverty, New Report Shows," *Humanosphere*, June 29, 2015, http://www.humanosphere.org/basics/2015/06/more-than-1-6-billion-people-live-in-poverty-says-index/.

22 "Global Multidimensional Poverty Index," Oxford Poverty & Human Development Initiative (OPHI), Oxford Department of International Development, 2018, https://ophi.org.uk/multidimensional-poverty-index/.

The health of a community is measured by two indicators: nutrition and child mortality. These are certainly not the only measures of health, but taken together they give insight into a community's knowledge of disease processes and prevention, their access to medical care, and the overall reality of food security.

The educational level of a community is also measured by two specific indicators: school attendance and the average number of years completed. This doesn't take into account the quality of the education, or the value of what is being taught to the context of the learner, but it is a start.

The third dimension—living standards—is measured by cooking fuel, sanitation, drinking water, electricity, flooring, and assets. These are valuable indicators for understanding the material deprivation of a community.

As research has advanced, OPHI has identified additional dimensions of poverty that weren't considered in the original study. These include quality of work, empowerment, physical safety, social connectedness, and psychological well-being.[23]

These studies are giving new definition to concepts of poverty on the world stage.[24] The World Bank's definition is giving way to a more wholistic way of looking at the problem of acute poverty. Poverty is complex, and real solutions require strategies that address all the hurdles the poor must overcome on their road to development.

Multidimensional definitions of poverty are proving undeniably that poverty is still a bigger problem than the World Bank's definition would indicate. For example, in Chad and Ethiopia the incidence of multidimensional poverty is about 87 percent, whereas using the World Bank's measure of $1.90/day poverty, it is only 37 percent.[25] Globally, the World Bank puts the number of people living in extreme poverty at 736 million.[26] Using the Multidimensional Index, OPHI puts the number at 1.6 billion, with 85 percent of the poor living in rural poor areas (villages).[27] The World Bank asserts that we have reduced extreme poverty globally to under 10 percent, but the Multidimensional Index puts the number of multidimensionally poor at almost 17 percent. The OPHI's Multidimensional Index, the statistics seem to show, is a more accurate measure.

The Multidimensional Poverty Index provides a fuller definition of poverty, but in my view it is still too narrow. Secular development programs often fail to address beliefs and values which we know to be essential to behavior change. True transformation begins in the heart and works itself out in life.

---

23 "Missing Dimensions," OPHI, https://ophi.org.uk/research/missing-dimensions/.

24 *Global Multidimensional Poverty.*

25 "Global MPI 2015: Key Findings." OPHI. https://ophi.org.uk/multidimensional-poverty-index/mpi-2015/.

26 "Decline of Global Extreme Poverty Continues but Has Slowed: World Bank," The World Bank website, September 19, 2018, https://www.worldbank.org/en/news/press-release/2018/09/19/decline-of-global-extreme-poverty-continues-but-has-slowed-world-bank.

27 "Global MPI 2018."

Bryant Myers, in his book *Walking with the Poor*, offers a definition of poverty anchored in the teaching of the Scriptures. He begins with the biblical assertion that human beings are made in the image of the triune God and intentionally placed in a system of relationships with God, self, others, and the environment. These relationships have been marred and distorted by sin, and no longer work for the well-being of the poor. As such, Myers proposes that "the nature of poverty is fundamentally relational, and that its cause is fundamentally spiritual."[28] If poverty is a result of broken relationships, then the process for alleviating poverty is a ministry of reconciliation.

Building on Myers' work, Brian Fikkert and Steve Corbett also define poverty as broken relationships with God, self, others, and the rest of creation. They identify four types of poverty that result from these broken relationships. The first flows from a broken relationship with God and is a "poverty of spiritual intimacy." The second is the result of broken relationships with others and is a "poverty of community." The third type of poverty comes out of a broken relationship with creation and is a "poverty of stewardship." Finally, the fourth type of poverty is broken relationship with one's self and results in a "poverty of being."[29]

Relationships with God and others must be taken into account when considering the primary factors contributing to deprivation. Broken relationships are often a cause for poverty and a roadblock to escaping from it. Conflict, corruption, disharmony, and a lack of concern for one another and for the common good are all barriers to progress. These must be overcome by positive relationships that include peace, cooperation, service to each other, and strong family ties.

In the same way, a community's worldview may also be a cause for poverty as well as a roadblock to escaping from it. Many times, people are trapped in poverty by lies that have been planted in their culture. These types of deceitful narratives promote values and behaviors, often indirectly, that are destructive to human development. For example, in much of the world women have limited access to education, possess a limited voice in decision-making, and are subject to all forms of abuse. This is because of certain cultural narratives that promote the idea that women are inferior to men.[30]

Another example of a bondage-inducing worldview is that of the Dalits in India. The Dalits are the lowest Hindu class and are therefore subject to all kinds of discrimination. The Hindu religious narrative defines the members of this social

---

28 *Global Multidimensional Poverty Index*. OPHI. http://ophi.org.uk/multidimensional-poverty-index/.

29 Brian Fikkert and Steve Corbett, *When Helping Hurts: How to Alleviate Poverty Without Hurting the Poor ... and Yourself* (Chicago: Moody, 2012), 61.

30 "Facts & Figures," UN Women website, 2012, http://www.unwomen.org/en/news/in-focus/commission-on-the-status-of-women-2012/facts-and-figures.

class as being unclean and untouchable. Such narratives hold the Dalits in poverty despite the numerous laws that have been passed to protect them.[31]

The solution to poverty is not merely providing what is missing materially. True transformation requires uprooting the lies that keep people in bondage, healing broken relationships, and working across the disciplines (health, development, education, psychology, etc.) to address the whole need of individuals and communities. That kind of framework or strategy is what I call "wholistic."

> **Wholistic ministry aims to bring the *whole* of life under the lordship of Christ and to reflect the values of the kingdom of God in our homes and communities.**

Wholistic Ministry: Meeting the Whole Need of Individuals and Communities

In light of the complexities of human poverty, transforming a community requires solutions to a whole range of issues that are essential to human flourishing: faith, family, water, wellness, agriculture, education, and income generation, to name a few. In the same way, development of the individual requires growth in every aspect of the human personality: social, spiritual, mental, and physical. Ministry that achieves transformation in lives, families, and communities must be wholistic—addressing the whole need of individuals and communities.

Wholistic ministry is a thoroughly biblical philosophy of ministry that aims at caring for the whole need of people and seeking the transformation of whole communities. I have deliberately chosen to add a "w" to the spelling of the word *holistic* in order to dispel notions of New Age ideology that can be carried by that word, especially in the realm of health and well-being. Wholistic ministry is about bringing the *whole* of life under the lordship of Christ and reflecting the values of the kingdom of God in our homes and communities.

---

31 "India's Dalits Still Fighting Untouchability," BBC News Services, June 27, 2012, https://www.bbc.com/news/world-asia-india-18394914.

CHAPTER 2

Accelerating Change for the Poor

Beyond Projects to Movements

Wholistic strategies that transform lives and communities in deep and noticeable ways create enthusiasm in transformed villages and attract the attention of the villages around them. When people in a village create real solutions using local resources and change the trajectory of their lives, they can spread their success to others and impact a cluster of villages around them. These dynamics create a "push" from the center and a "pull" from the periphery, thus making it possible for change to multiply from village to village. If others in the cluster become models that multiply, a movement is born.

Launching these types of movements all around the globe puts transformation in a million villages within reach. It will, however, require significant changes in our ministry paradigms. We will need to go beyond doing things for people to empowering people to do things for themselves. We will need to engage with villagers as active participants rather than passive recipients in the work and spread of gospel transformation. We will need to equip our congregations to be movement-makers rather than just project planners.

> Transformational movements multiply change from village to village, improving the quality and trajectory of life for an entire region.

These may seem like monumental shifts in the way we think and operate and in the kind of outcomes we expect—and they are. Hopefully, though, after reading this book you will have some clarity about how to launch a transformational movement and will be able to mark out a clear path to getting it done.

I am using the word *movement* in the book to describe the multiplication of change from village to village by villagers. In order to claim that we have launched a true movement, we must see at least four generations of change—change that continues to multiply beyond the context of those who first initiated it.[32]

---

[32] Roy Moran, "Disciple Making Movements—a History and a Definition," Discipleship.org, https://discipleship.org/bobbys-blog/disciple-making-movements-part-1/.

Transformational movements are deep, wide, and long. They are *deep* in that the change is significant, changing the quality and trajectory of life. The change impacts life at every level: beliefs, values, behaviors, individuals, families, and communities. Transformational movements are *wide* in that there are multiple streams of transformation flowing at the same time within and across ethnic and national boundaries. They are *long* in that what is initiated continues to multiply over time.

A Proven Strategy

> Community Health Evangelism (CHE) brings people to faith in Christ while lifting whole communities out of cycles of poverty and disease.

In 1997 I was introduced to Community Health Evangelism (CHE), a wholistic ministry strategy for ministry to the poor. At the time, CHE was being taught and used by Medical Ambassadors International, based in Modesto, California. Those using the strategy strove to obey everything Jesus commanded, including both the Great Commission and the Great Commandment, and envisioned lives and communities transformed by the power of the gospel. I was attracted to their ministry and joined their ranks. Eventually God led me to serve these workers as their international coordinator and later to establish the Global CHE Network.

The CHE strategy is now being used by network members from more than 950 organizations in 136 countries and has become a global movement. The stories I will tell and the principles I will articulate in the chapters that follow are from my travel diaries as a leader in the CHE movement. I share them in a spirit of collaboration, hoping that what we, as a global network of CHE workers, have learned will inspire and equip you to begin transformational movements that spread from village to village and country to country, changing the lives of the village poor forever.

Community Health Evangelism (CHE) seamlessly integrates Christian discipleship with disease prevention and community-owned development. It is a Christ-centered educational program that equips communities to identify issues and mobilize resources in order to achieve positive, sustainable change. Lives and communities are transformed as people come to Christ and work together to address local needs. Through CHE ministries, people become followers of Jesus and whole communities are lifted out of cycles of poverty and disease.

When a CHE program is mature, volunteer health workers called Community Health Evangelists (CHEs) visit homes and work with families. They teach about both physical and spiritual topics. For example, they may teach about the importance of clean water and help families to sanitize their drinking water.

At the same time, they open the Scriptures and teach about the Living Water. Those who come to Christ gather in small groups for fellowship, worship, Bible study, and prayer.

The CHEs report to a development committee made up of leaders elected by the community to manage the development process. The committee members initiate and manage projects of their choosing, such as immunization, water, sanitation, infrastructure, schools, agriculture, micro enterprise development, and programs for women and youth. All the volunteers in the organization within the community (the development committee and the CHEs) are trained by "trainers," usually nationals living in a nearby city or town who are equipped with simple strategies for raising awareness and mobilizing a community to work together.

The Million Village Challenge

The concept of movements rather than projects was built into the DNA of CHE by its founder, Stan Rowland. One of his core principles was multiplication. He wasn't content to do projects that impacted just a single village, but intentionally worked to start movements with the potential to sweep the countryside. The result of his laser-like focus was a ministry strategy that resulted in transformational movements. From its early beginnings in a small rural community in Uganda in 1980, the CHE movement has multiplied into 136 different countries—and it is still growing.[33]

As Stan's successor at Medical Ambassadors and as founder of the Global CHE Network, I have been privileged to watch the spread of CHE and to witness the multiplication of wholistic change up close. Transformational movements have been catalyzed, and change has spread from village to village and country to country, making disciples of Christ while lifting communities out of cycles of poverty and disease. I am convinced that if churches and faith-based organizations around the globe move beyond doing projects to movements, we can bring new life to a million villages.

This book is intended to cast vision for the task that needs to be done among the world's poorest and to lay out a strategy for doing it. The idea of the Million Village Challenge is to lift our eyes to the magnitude of the task that is before us and get to work.

The vision for change in a million villages is a vision for the church globally. It is a way of visualizing opportunities that will make a difference for the advance of the kingdom at a moment when the church is uniquely positioned to seize them. Our vision is to equip a vast army of people from within the church, motivated by love and compassion, to alleviate poverty, release the oppressed, heal

---
[33] Global CHE Network homepage, https://www.chenetwork.org.

the sick, and proclaim the good news of the gospel in a million villages. Together we will plant churches while helping poor communities break free from cycles of poverty and despair. Our ultimate aim is to bring glory to their Father in heaven and exalt his name throughout the earth.

In this book, I will share the biblical foundations for transformational ministry, identify underlying principles essential to transformational movements, and lay out a path to help you move beyond projects to wholistic gospel movements that will change the lives of the village poor forever.

CHAPTER 3: Change Begins Here

The Gospel of the Kingdom

Jesus preached what Matthew describes as the "gospel of the kingdom" (Matt 24:14). His ministry embraced the concerns of justice and compassion and promised not just a personal, private relationship with God, but a vision to see God's kingdom come on earth as it is in heaven (Matt 6:10). This gospel of the kingdom would be a "testimony to all nations" (Matt 24:14; see also Matt 3:2; 4:23).

Jesus came not only to save souls, but to redeem everything that was broken by the fall. Jesus came to offer his life as an atoning sacrifice for our sins, and he will come again to reign in the new heaven and the new earth, where there will be no more death or crying or pain. The end of the story is the restoration of the human condition and a return to life as God intends it to be. Jesus did not come just to forgive sins, but to restore the human condition in all its aspects. The story ends not just with our rescue from condemnation, but entrance into the kingdom of God.

The restoration of the human condition begins with a new birth, forgiveness of sins, and restored fellowship with God through faith in Christ. This new birth and renewed fellowship with God find expression in individuals (believers, disciples) and communities (churches) that reflect the values of the kingdom, which Jesus preached. Our lives and ministries, therefore, should reflect the depth and breadth of his kingdom plan. Our purpose as his followers, if indeed we share his purpose, is bigger than evangelism; it is a call to make disciples who obey everything Jesus commanded, and to reflect the values of the kingdom he came to establish. The kingdom of God is present in us, but it will find its fulfillment in the new heaven and the new earth when Jesus comes again.

Jesus preached a message of forgiveness and eternal life. He also proclaimed righteousness, peace, justice and reconciliation in the present. The message of the kingdom, as Jesus declared it, has implications for the present *and* for the future. It is salvation for sinners and good news to the poor. God invites the hungry and homeless, the sick and the prisoner, the

> **Jesus came not only to save souls, but to redeem everything that was broken by the fall.**

economically poor and the socially powerless, to feast at his table. He says to them, in essence, "I love you, and you are welcome to my party" (Luke 4:16–21).

> Biblical transformation is the quiet work of the Holy Spirit in the heart of the believer, and it is the loud sounding of the trumpet at the second coming of Christ.

As followers of Jesus, we have all experienced the transforming power of God at work in us—that quiet work of the Holy Spirit convicting us of wrongdoing, cleansing our hearts, shaping our character, changing our attitudes, and influencing our actions. We also look forward to a time when our lives and communities are completely transformed in the new heaven and the new earth. Biblical transformation is that *quiet* work of the Holy Spirit in the heart of the believer, and it is the *loud* sounding of the trumpet at the return of the Lord Jesus—shutting up evil and establishing righteousness, justice, and peace for all eternity.

The biblical concept of transformation is both an intensely personal relationship with God and a just and compassionate social order. It is more than simply a personal relationship with God that transforms our inner life, but rather a complete regeneration of our being, thinking, and doing that works itself out in our friendships, families, and communities.

There is a present as well as a future aspect to this biblical transformation. We are growing in love, righteousness, and holiness, but we will not be fully like Christ until he comes again (1 John 3:2). In the same way, we work for peace, righteousness, and justice, but we will not see the fullness of the kingdom of God until Jesus returns as judge and king.

The Pharisees once asked Jesus *when* the kingdom would come. He replied by saying, "The kingdom of God *is* among you" (Luke 17:21 NRSV; emphasis mine). The kingdom of God is present now. It is present when Christian people in the name of Jesus act to release the poor in the developing world from cycles of poverty and disease. It is present when relief is offered in the name of Christ to victims of a tsunami. It is present when the poor participate in decisions which affect their lives and gain access to resources and knowledge. It is present when Christians help to alleviate poverty. It is present when forgiveness of sins is proclaimed, and Jesus is acknowledged as Lord.

For many years, I believed the sole purpose of the miracles Jesus performed was to prove his power and identity. Jesus' miracles demonstrated that he was the Christ, the Son of God. He raised Lazarus from the dead and then declared, "I am the resurrection and the life" (John 11:25). He said, "I am the light of the world" (John 9:5), and then healed a blind man (John 9:6–34). Jesus' miracles demonstrated his power over nature, demons, sickness, and death.

I have come to believe the miracles of Jesus not only revealed his power, but that they also portrayed his purpose. The miracles of Jesus were a demonstration of *who* he is and *what* he came to do. By his miracles, Jesus demonstrated that he came to forgive sins (Matt 9:4-6); give eternal life (John 11:25); heal the sick and drive out demons (Mark 1:34); calm storms (Mark 8:24); feed the hungry (Matt 14:2); free captives from oppression (Mark 12:9–14); cleanse disease (Matt 8:1–4); unite the peoples of the earth (Matt 8:5–13); and bring in the kingdom of God (Matt 12:28).

Jesus systematically taught about the character and morality of those who inherit the kingdom (Matt 5–7). He spoke directly to the moral issues of his day: murder, adultery, divorce, oaths, vengeance, love for enemies, giving to the needy, prayer and fasting, materialism, judging others, and hypocrisy. He summed up his teaching with the Golden Rule: "In everything, do to others what you would have them do to you, for this sums up the Law and the Prophets" (Matt 7:12).

When talking about the character and morals of his followers, Jesus also speaks of their influence. Followers of Jesus who inherit the kingdom will have enormous influence on the world in which they live. He tells his followers that they are the light of the world and the salt of the earth—God's transforming agents in a dark and decaying world. The application seems obvious: As we develop the character of Christ and apply his teaching to our lives, we reflect kingdom values that have the potential to transform the communities in which we live.

Jesus taught us to pray, "Your kingdom come, your will be done, on earth as it is in heaven" (Matt 6:10). This is the goal of wholistic ministry. Transformation is God's kingdom work: It is a process and an ideal, a present experience and a future hope, a means and an end, a struggle and a victory. God is at work among us today, and he will bring what he has started to completion when the Lord Jesus returns in all his glory. We will not know the fullness of the kingdom until our Lord comes again, but *the king is here, and his kingdom is among us.*

God always transforms from the inside out—his work begins in our hearts and works itself out in our lives. He works *in us,* then *through us,* then *among us.* Our journey is a transforming journey toward a more transformational ministry.

As we change, our churches will change too. We will move beyond performances and programs that attract a crowd, to bold and righteous living that transforms our communities. We will gain credibility with people, and a disproportionate influence in society. We will become what Jesus said we are, the light of the world and the salt of the earth. This will be the beginning of change for a million villages.

Complete Obedience to Everything Jesus Commanded

As I mentioned in the introduction, when Jeannie and I arrived on the mission field as young missionaries, a veteran pulled me aside with a single word of advice, which summarized the philosophy of ministry of my new colleagues: "If you feed somebody today, they will be hungry again tomorrow. If you save their soul today, they will be saved forever." His words were consistent with what the majority of evangelicals at that time believed about the mission of the church. We hadn't come to the Philippines to care for the people's physical needs, but to preach and plant churches.

As a group of missionaries, we thought about our Christian faith almost exclusively in terms of a personal relationship with God and fellowship with his people. Our faith was about receiving forgiveness of sins and a place in heaven. We didn't connect our faith with justice and compassion or doing our part to contribute to the earthly needs of the poor. The result of this dichotomy was that we planted churches without a social conscience. We taught new Christians to pray, read their Bible, and witness. We taught them to attend church, to get baptized, and to use their spiritual gifts. We taught them to give to the Lord's work, and to be good stewards of their time and money. We taught them to meditate on God's Word and to resist temptation.

> **Followers of Jesus are the light of the world—God's transforming agents in a dark and decaying world.**

In spite of all of these positive practices, however, the new believers were not engaged at all in regard to compassion for the poor. The tragic outcome of this for our churches was that we eventually became marginalized and isolated from the community. All we brought to the table from the perspective of the communities we were serving was a theological argument.

I would have argued back then that the weightiest command of Jesus was the command to save souls, and that this should be the single mission of the church. I would have backed up that argument by saying it doesn't matter how many good things we do for a person if, in the end, that person spends eternity in hell.

I can no longer make that argument. I had to repent of that mindset. I was prioritizing the commands of Christ rather than finding a way to obey everything he commanded. I needed to stop choosing which of Christ's commands I would obey and find a way to be obedient to everything he commanded. When Jesus commissioned his followers to make disciples, he followed the command immediately with a clear statement of what that would require—baptizing them and teaching them to obey *everything* Jesus commanded (Matt 28:19–20).

In the chapters to follow, I will tell the stories of different followers of Jesus in rural poor village communities around the world who are bringing life, health, and hope to their own people. Their ministries testify to the power of the gospel to transform individual lives and to lift whole communities out of cycles of poverty and disease. They are committed to complete obedience to everything Jesus commanded, and to living out their faith in word and deed. They bring the message of forgiveness of sins and eternal life through faith in Christ, and they display a love that acts in the interest of their neighbors. As a result, people are coming to

Christ, churches are being planted, and communities are being transformed. Their stories will inspire us to want to imitate their faith, while the values and principles from which they operate will challenge us to rethink how we "do ministry."

> Instead of prioritizing the commands of Christ, we need to find a way to obey everything Christ commanded.

Crossing the Sacred-Secular Divide

Scott Allen, in his book *Beyond the Sacred-Secular Divide*, describes a problem that limits the ministry of the church and its impact in the community. He says,

> Many Christians today live in two worlds—the "spiritual" world of faith and the church, and the "secular" world of work and daily life. In so dividing their lives, they reduce Christianity to a series of religious meetings and church-based programs. Their Christian faith is privately engaging but irrelevant to their social, economic, or political concerns.[34]

In other words, if the Lord Jesus is not at the very center of everything we do, then health care, agriculture, business, education, politics, art, and entertainment can be "secular" vocations. However, if Jesus is Lord of every aspect of our lives, we cannot segment our lives into the "secular" and the "sacred." Providing healing through health care, food through agriculture, shelter through enterprise, or wisdom through education is as much a "ministry" as teaching a Bible study or preaching a sermon.

The sacred-secular divide is a form of dualism that allows us to live under the lordship of Christ in one realm while living according to the values and norms of our culture in another. We do the work of the Lord by attending church, reading our Bibles, praying, and worshiping on Sunday. We work for a living (money) the rest of the week. The sad consequence of our dualism is a faith that informs our religious traditions but does not inform our values, change our behaviors, or transform our lives and communities. It becomes difficult to distinguish a believer from an unbeliever, and the church loses its capacity as God's transforming agent in society. If we want transformed lives and communities, then we need an integrated approach to life and ministry that unites all things under the lordship of Christ.

> The change we envision in a million villages is wholistic change that puts Christ at the center of everything from education and economic development to social concerns and family life.

Allen goes on to propose that the solution to the sacred-secular divide is wholism:

---
34 Scott Allen, *Beyond the Sacred-Secular Divide* (Seattle: YWAM Publishing, 2011), 41–45.

A wholistic life is one lived in complete submission to God, not just in "spiritual" things, but in everything. If my commitment to the Lord Jesus exists at the very center of everything I do, my life has integrity. My faith unites the parts of my life into a greater whole, with all the parts giving glory to God.[35]

The change we envision in a million villages is wholistic change—change that puts Christ at the center of everything from education and economic development to social concerns and family life. The purpose of our work in villages is to exalt Christ in every aspect of life. Our strategy includes discipleship and church planting, disease prevention, and poverty alleviation. Our vision is a transformation in lives and communities that is as deep as the human heart and as broad as the whole range of the human experience in the world God made. Through our work, Jesus is recognized as Lord over all creation, and our activities bring glory to God by reflecting the depth and breadth of his kingdom plan.

The Church as God's Agent of Transformation

In Matthew 5:14–16, Jesus made an astounding affirmation regarding the identity and mission of the church—about who we are as his followers and what he intends for us to do. Jesus said to his followers, "You are the light of the world" (Matt 5:14). With that, he is basically saying, "You are my chosen agent of transformation. Through you I will change the world." He did not say that as flattery; rather, he said it because it's true. We are the light of the world and the hope of the nations—God's agent of transformation.

In addition, the word *you* in the original Greek is plural. Jesus is not saying that you, individually, are the light of the world, but that we, collectively as the church, are the light of the world. *The church is God's agent of transformation.* While each of us individually has a role to play, it takes all of us collectively to influence cultures and heal nations.

At a "Finishing the Task" conference at Saddleback Church which I attended in 2015, Pastor Rick Warren argued that "the church is the answer to every problem on the planet." The church, he said, has "the largest standing volunteer army in the world—by a factor of 100." Warren claimed that this army, because of its size and distribution, can do what needs to be done faster than any government, nonprofit agency, or business on earth.[36] He followed these bold statements with the following story.

In 2005, *Time* magazine reported that Warren had been asked by Rwandan president, Paul Kagame, to help his country become a "purpose-driven nation."[37] Working with leaders of business and leaders of parliament, Warren sent 1,400

---

35 Ibid.
36 Rick Warren, Finishing the Task conference, December 2015, https://vimeo.com/152312181.
37 David Van Biema, "Warren of Rwanda," *Time*, August 15, 2005.

Saddleback Church members with specific expertise to Rwanda to train and equip leaders from all sectors for a national strategy. At the same time, he enlisted the cooperation of six hundred Rwandan churches. I was invited to Saddleback Church in Lake Forest, California, along with two of my colleagues from Medical Ambassadors International (MAI) to record twenty-six training videos for equipping these volunteers.

> "The church is the answer to every problem on the planet."
> – Rick Warren

Their plan for Rwanda was called P.E.A.C.E., an acrostic that described the areas in which they would focus their work: **P**lant churches that promote reconciliation; **E**quip servant leaders; **A**ssist the poor; **C**are for the sick; and **E**ducate the next generation.

In 2006, Warren was invited to be the closing speaker at the first ever White House Summit on Malaria, which was dedicated to the elimination of malaria in Africa. According to the summit's fact sheet, more than a million infants and children under five in sub-Saharan Africa died each year from the mosquito-borne disease. Groups like the Bill & Melinda Gates Foundation, Exxon Mobil, the Global Fund, Malaria No More, and Saddleback Church rose to President Bush's challenge of mobilizing private sector support to defeat malaria in Africa.[38]

Warren agreed to come on the condition that he could bring pastors from Rwanda. He wanted to prove the work that needs to be done regarding malaria prevention and eradication can be done faster by the church than by any government agency, NGO, or business. At the Global Summit on Malaria, Warren spoke to an elite group of people. He began his presentation by challenging them, saying, "I'm going to show you how we can do what needs to be done faster by local churches than by anybody here—I don't care how much money you have."

He then went on to display a series of three slides, maps of the Western Province of Rwanda, where there were about 700,000 people and just one doctor. There were hospitals and clinics, but only one qualified doctor in the entire province. This was the region where President Kagame specifically asked Warren to "care for the sick." These maps visualized the available health care assets that could be identified locally. The first slide had only three dots on it, representing the three hospitals in that area of the country. Warren reminded those attending the summit that since there was only one doctor in the province, chances were thin that any one of the two million people would see him, even if they could get to the hospital. He concluded the first slide by saying, "By the way, two of the three hospitals in this province are church-based: The Seventh Day Adventists established one, and the Presbyterians another. So, you wouldn't have two of the three hospitals if it weren't for the church."

---

38 https://georgewbush-whitehouse.archives.gov/news/releases/2006/12/20061214.html.

> While each of us individually has a role to play, it takes all of us collectively to influence cultures and heal nations.

Warren then projected a second map of the province, this one with eighteen dots, each of which represented an operating clinic. "This is better than three hospitals," he said, "because a clinic can be found within less than a day's walk from any village. But many of the clinics are just a bottle of aspirin on a shelf." He went on to say that sixteen of the eighteen clinics were also church based. "You wouldn't have those sixteen clinics if it weren't for the church."

Finally, Warren showed the audience a third slide with a map that was covered with dots. "Here are the 867 churches in the province." Then he asked, "Where would you rather get your health care? A two days' walk, a one day's walk, or five minutes away?"[39]

After his speech, Melinda Gates approached Warren and said, "I get it, Rick. The church can be the distribution for health care." Warren replied, "Melinda, it has been for two thousand years. The church invented the hospital."

Warren then hired one of my colleagues from MAI, Dr. Gil Odendaal, to direct the P.E.A.C.E. program in the Western Province, using the Community Health Evangelism (CHE) approach and materials. Over the next five years, Gil and his team trained and mobilized about five thousand Rwandan nationals as volunteer health workers. These workers made house calls. They taught families how to prevent disease with clean water, sanitation, and hygiene. They taught them to eat nutritious foods and grow FAITH (**Food Always in The Home**) gardens, to do basic first aid, and to ward off malaria. They also taught about Jesus, the Living Water, and discipled people they served within small groups.

In August of 2014, Warren returned to Rwanda and hosted a rally celebrating the achievement of the church. All five thousand volunteers wore colored T-shirts, identifying themselves with the church they attended. The achievements were significant enough that after the celebration Warren received invitations from the presidents of six other African countries: Nigeria, the Democratic Republic of Congo, Malawi, Liberia, Burundi, and Sierra Leone. The global church is uniquely positioned to meet some of the biggest challenges in the world today. In many remote places, the church is the only institution with the capacity to do what needs to be done.

Let me share a story from Zambia that also demonstrates the potential impact of the church on a nation. This time the champion was not a megachurch pastor, but an ordinary young couple, Lovemore and Mavis, who lived in a small hut in

---

39 Rick Warren, Finishing the Task conference, December 2015, https://vimeo.com/152312181.
    Warren said similar things in this interview in 2009, HYPERLINK "https://www.pewforum.org/2009/11/13/the-future-of-evangelicals-a-conversation-with-pastor-rick-warren/"https://www.pewforum.org/2009/11/13/the-future-of-evangelicals-a-conversation-with-pastor-rick-warren/#11.

the city of Lusaka. They had no vehicle, so they used public transportation and walked everywhere they needed to go.

Lovemore received training in CHE from a couple of missionaries from the Assemblies of God. When God called these missionaries to move on, they entrusted Lovemore with a fledgling work in three villages, some of them more than twelve miles away from where he lived. Lovemore felt called to continue the work, even if he had to do it alone and without many resources.

Lovemore's legacy includes a network of churches in Zambia that have mobilized workers in ten provinces. On several occasions, I spoke with leaders Lovemore had trained and visited communities he had organized. Volunteers diversified and improved agriculture, taught disease prevention, championed ministry to the disabled, and multiplied micro-enterprise development.

The president of Zambia, Edgar Luna, was so impressed by Lovemore's work that he invited him to serve on his cabinet as a deputy minister for community health and development. Lovemore politely turned the president down, saying "I will work with you, but not for you." He recognized that the work belonged to the church, not to the government.

In December of 2017, I was invited to speak, along with the minister of health at the formal launch and ribbon-cutting ceremony of Lovemore's new NGO, the Community Health Evangelism and Education Program. The minister praised Lovemore for his contribution to the nation's health and development goals.

In October of 2018, I received the sad news that Lovemore had gone to be with his Lord. There is a huge soccer stadium outside of Lusaka, where Lovemore lived, that seats perhaps seventy thousand people. Every time we drove by it together, I would tell Lovemore that one day he was going fill that stadium with his volunteers and have a grand celebration of what God had done through them. I am praying now, as I write, that God will use his testimony and legacy as recorded here to inspire many champions like him in countries all around the world to rise up and initiate transformational movements among the village poor.

These two stories, first in Rwanda, then in Zambia, illustrate the change that the church can bring to communities and nations. The church is God's agent of transformation. Change that God intends is anchored in the teaching of Jesus and the gospel of the kingdom. It works itself out through the church, as followers of Jesus obey everything Jesus commanded, including the Great Commission and the Great Commandment.

CHAPTER 4 Changing Together

Looking Beyond the Wheelchair

Someone has said, "The worst thing about a disability is that people see it before they see you." Advocates for the disabled communicate this sad reality in different ways. Here is a poem gleaned from the internet that communicates the need for able-bodied people to look beyond the wheelchair:

> Not a label. Not a Word. Not a derogatory term you heard.
>
> I'm a who. Same as you. Do you have a name? . . . Me too.
>
> I'm a mind. A heart. A personality. I'm an equal part of the overall we.
>
> I'm a him or a her. A he or a she.
>
> Who am I? I'm simply me. A person. Not a disability.[40]

Disabled individuals want to be valued as contributors—to be given access to our structures and institutions, to be given a place in the workforce, to have the opportunity to use their skills and abilities to provide for themselves and their families. One person put it this way:

> See my disability. Discourage me. Discount me.
>
> See my ability. Encourage me. Count me in.[41]

The cry of the poor and disabled often echo each other. *When those who are able-bodied or materially wealthy focus on others' needs and overlook their strengths and abilities, they treat them as projects rather than people.* In the process, they deprive them of dignity, worth, and opportunity.

My experience teaches me that people in extreme poverty show unimaginable strength and endurance as they persist in overcoming the hardships of extreme poverty. They exhibit incredible ingenuity and resourcefulness in everyday living. Poor and/or disabled people are some of the strongest human beings I have ever met.

---

[40] The Center for Family Support website, https://www.cfsny.org/thank-you-for-supporting-our-self-advocates/.
[41] Source unknown.

We need to begin our journey with the economically poor by reflecting on our prejudiced attitudes toward them. We must see them as active participants and not passive recipients in their development process. We must see them as stewards of resources rather than victims of circumstance, as subjects rather than objects of development activities, as teachers as well as learners, and senders as well as receivers. Let's look at each of these notions one at a time.

Stewards Rather Than Victims

The economically poor often see themselves as victims of circumstance rather than as stewards of resources. However, the clear teaching of the Bible is just the opposite. Human beings were created to have dominion over creation, not to be dominated by it. They are above creation—not equal to creation, one with creation, or below creation. People have been commissioned by their Creator to manage and cultivate the garden in which he placed them.

Immediately after creating Adam and Eve, God blessed the couple and said to them: "Be fruitful and increase in number; fill the earth and subdue it. Rule over the fish of the sea and the birds of the air and over every living creature that moves on the ground" (Gen 1:28). He then put them in the Garden of Eden "to work it and take care of it" (Gen 2:15).

> **Transformational development is more than improving yields and lengthening life. It restores dignity, purpose, and vocation in the human person.**

The truth that humans were created as stewards is empowering. The fact that we have been given dominion over the resources God has supplied in the earth gives us hope and vision for a better quality of life. It inspires innovation, creativity, and ingenuity. It motivates us to work to gather the full benefit from what God has entrusted to our care. It frees the mind from fatalistic notions and passive acceptance of life in an impoverished state. But most importantly, it is foundational to progress and development.

Any belief that contradicts the truth that we are made in the image of God and stewards of the earth's resources is disempowering. When people are captive to such beliefs, progress is ultimately hindered and human development is stunted. One concrete example of a belief system that contradicts this truth is animism.

Animism, as I am using it here, is the idea that spirits control the material world and have power over such things as harvest, health, and general well-being. Villagers all over the world are taken captive by animistic worldview assumptions. The major religions which villagers profess—Christianity, Islam, Hinduism, and Buddhism—are often just a veneer over deeply held animistic beliefs. This syncretism of beliefs is classified, by those who study it, as "Folk Religion";

and with 405 million adherents, it is the fifth-largest religious demographic in the world.[42] "Folk Christianity" describes the blending of traditional beliefs and practices such as magic, witchcraft, and voodoo with Christian faith and doctrine. "Folk Islam" describes the same phenomenon in Muslim countries. People living in rural poor villages all around the world are victims of this deception.

From the perspective of community development, animism hinders progress by perpetuating a belief that the assets of a community don't belong to the people, but to spirits and gods. A vision to steward the assets of their community and create solutions to the problems they face is subverted by a sense of dependency and a need to use ritual sacrifices, magic, and witchcraft to manipulate the favor of gods and spirits. These belief systems have significant implications for community development, especially when proposed changes are viewed to upset the equilibrium in the spirit world.

I've already mentioned the village in Northern Thailand where the elders rejected the government's attempts to pipe clean water into every home because the pipes would anger the spirits. In another village in the same area, pigs donated to the community for income generation and food security were slaughtered as a sacrificial offering to ancestral spirits rather than being allowed to give birth and multiply. There can be no physical development in these situations without a corresponding change in the people's worldview assumptions.

As those sent to serve the poor, the last thing we want to do is reinforce a belief system that leaves the poor passive and dependent, believing they are victims rather than stewards. However, the hard truth is that we have often approached the poor as if they were victims, sharing their opinion that they cannot do anything for themselves. We have done this by making poor people our projects—objects of *our* development work rather than actors in *their own* development process. If we want to see change in a million villages, then villagers must become owners and champions of their own development rather than passive recipients in outsiders' development projects.

> If we want to see change in a million villages, then villagers must become owners and champions of their own development, and agents of change for villages around them.

---

42 "Folk Religionists," Pew Research Center website, December 18, 2012, https://www.pewforum.org/2012/12/18/global-religious-landscape-folk/.

Subjects Rather Than Objects

Robert Chambers, an academic and practitioner in international development, has been one of the leading advocates for putting the poor at the center of the development process. In his 1983 work *Rural Development: Putting the Last First*, he introduced what he called a "new professionalism in international development."[43] He explained how the old professionalism had failed to alleviate poverty and argued that a new approach was needed.

The old professionalism, according to Chambers, is a blueprinted approach to working with the poor. Educated people from the centers of power act independently of the community they are "bettering." It is the outsider who assesses the needs, diagrams the solutions, raises the funds, hires the staff, implements the programs, and evaluates the outcomes and impact. The poor are merely objects of development.

In contrast, Chambers' new professionalism involves the poor working together to solve their own problems. They assess their own needs, choose their own priorities, create their own solutions, identify their own resources, and change their own communities. In this way, the poor remain the subjects rather than the objects of the development process. This perspective is consistent with God's attitude and desires for the economically poor. Transformational development is not just about improving yields and lengthening life. It is also about restoring dignity, purpose, and vocation in the human person.

Unfortunately, much of the work we have been doing as missionaries has been built on the assumption that the poor are objects of development. We have believed that we can lift the poor out of poverty by doing things for them. This couldn't be further from the truth. The escape from poverty will only be at the initiative of the poor themselves. The poor must be the subjects rather than the objects of development.

Teachers as Well as Learners

I met Jesus in the village. I'm not saying that the village is where I first heard about Jesus, or even where I gave my heart to him. But the village is where I learned the meaning of many of Jesus' words and the priorities of his heart. There I saw his values at work, transforming lives and communities in ways I have not seen in my North American neighborhood.

Some of the wealthiest people I know are economically poor. They go without a meal now and then, but they know God and they love each other. They live in communities that are rich with relationship and where they share a sense of belonging. They use their time, resources, skills, and abilities to help one another.

---

43 Robert W. Chambers, *Rural Development: Putting the Last First* (Abingdon, UK: Routledge, 1983).

There was a time in rural America when we knew our neighbors and used our knowledge and skills to help each other. We had porches and sat out front chatting with people as they passed by. If we needed a cake, we knew Susie made delicious creations, so we would talk to her about flavor, icing, and design options. And everyone knew Joe could fix our plumbing problems, or that Mike understood the mechanics of our vehicles.

In suburban neighborhoods today, however, we don't know our neighbors anymore. We have backyards instead of porches. We approach our homes inside a vehicle, and park inside our garage. We seldom talk with the people who live next door. Oftentimes we don't even know their names.

Life in the city is more transactional than relational. We all go to school, learn a skill or a service, and then market our products and services to each other. As a result, when we have a need we no longer visit our neighbor for help; instead, we go somewhere to buy a service.

Church life in the city is often not much different. We go to church and sit in rows beside total strangers. We recognize some of the people we worship with, but know little of consequence about them. Our pastor and his team deliver a "service," and we pay our tithe in the offering plate. If the services offered by the church are not to our liking, we shop around for a better product. This is often our experience, but it's not what Jesus intended for his church.

Life is not like that in the village. Villagers generally live in rich relationship, exchanging goods and services and depending on each other. In many ways, their way of life reflects the ideals Jesus modeled for his disciples. Consider the evening in the Upper Room, recorded for us in John 13, when Jesus washed his disciples' feet, and then later that night was arrested.

I've tried to put myself in Jesus' place that night. If I knew I would soon be tortured and suffer a painful death, that one of my closest friends was about to deny me, and that another friend was about to betray me, I doubt that I would have knelt down to wash their feet. I'm almost certain I would have stood up and fought for self-preservation. At a time when all of us would be inclined to stand up and fight, Jesus knelt down and served, expressing his deep love for his friends.

Knowing he was facing the cross, Jesus was most anxious to show the disciples the full extent of his love by washing their feet, as well as setting an example for them of how they should treat each other. When he had finished washing their feet, Jesus concluded by saying, "I have set you an example that you should do as I have done for you …. Now that you know these things, you will be *blessed* if you do them" (John 13:15, 17). The lesson for the evening was this: Those who live in intimate relationship and express their love for each other by acts of humble service will be "blessed," or "happy."

> **We are blind to our own poverty while we are focused on theirs.**

Many people living with an abundance of material possessions know little of the richness of relation-ship Jesus intends for his people. We see ourselves as blessed because of our many belongings, and we think of those with less of this world's goods as poor and unhappy. The truth is that we would be better off to miss an occasional meal than to walk through life independent and alone. There is richness and wisdom in a simpler way of life which we have not yet understood. We are blind to our own poverty while we are focused on theirs.

There is much we can learn from villagers who rely on God every day to provide their next meal. "Has not God chosen those who are poor in the eyes of the world to be rich in faith and to inherit the kingdom he promised those who love him?" (James 2:5). If the economically poor are rich in faith and heirs of the kingdom, they certainly have as much to teach us as we do them.

Our journey into their world is an opportunity to learn and grow. But we must stop doing projects long enough to listen. Do you hear the call? We are being invited: "Come, meet Jesus in the village. Sit at the feet of villagers and listen as they reveal the meaning of Jesus' words and the priorities of his heart."

SENDERS AS WELL AS RECEIVERS

Back in 1994, I served as a volunteer at the Philippine Mission Association (PMA). I became part of a task force set up to help mobilize Filipino Overseas Contract Workers (OCWs) as "tent-making missionaries"—missionaries who support themselves by working full-time in the marketplace while still dedicated to evangelistic ministry. The origin for the word comes from the Apostle Paul, who supported himself by being a tent-maker (Acts 18:1–4). We called our project Global Intent.

While mission agencies around the world were trying to get their people into restricted-access nations, Filipino Christians were already there! A former Director for Unreached Peoples at the U.S. Center for World Mission told me that at the time Filipino OCWs were one of the greatest untapped resources for finishing the task of world evangelization.

Government estimates indicated there were 795,000 Filipinos working abroad in 1994.[44] Bound for North America and the Middle East, two thousand Filipinos were leaving their homeland every day. By 2013 the number of Filipinos working abroad had grown to 10.2 million—one of the largest diaspora populations, spread across more than a hundred countries![45]

---

44 "Press Release on the 1996 Overseas Filipino Workers," Philippine Statistics Authority, https://psa.gov.ph/content/press-release-1996-overseas-filipino-workers.

45 https://psa.gov.ph/content/press-release-1996-overseas-filipino-workers.

In November of 1995, Global Intent sponsored the first set of national tent-making seminars in the Philippines: one in Manila and one in Davao. Some of the participants were bound for thirteen different restricted-access nations; others were preparing to go to various other countries.

The obvious next step was to provide basic training for the tent-making missionaries who were being mobilized through the seminars. A course titled "Basic Training for Tent-making Missionaries" (BTTM) was developed with the goal of giving OCWs general information concerning tent-making strategies and cross-cultural ministry, as well as to help them make a personal plan for getting the training and support they needed to do the job effectively. Twenty-one people enrolled in the first BTTM seminar.

The idea that Filipino contract workers could serve as tent-making missionaries sparked the imagination of the Philippine church. Far East Broadcasting Company (FEBC) broad-cast some of the sessions from the first national tent-making seminar on their network of stations. *Evangelicals Today* (a Philippine publication) dedicated their entire March issue in 1996 to the OCW and tent-making missions. I was invited to be a contributing author for several articles. Churches began to set up programs to train their own overseas workers for missionary work. The PMA helped sponsor the first National Youth Missions Congress. Global Intent oversaw the tent-making track. More than 1,100 young people attended from all over the Philippines, with an estimated 300 of those having already committed themselves to going to the mission field.

Nearly fifteen years later, in September of 2011, I traveled back to Manila to speak at an international conference. I was given the opportunity to meet with Pastor Nono Badoy, the new executive director for what used to be Global Intent but had since been renamed the Philippine Mission Mobilization Movement (PM3). He reported that more than fifty thousand Overseas Filipino Workers had been mobilized as tent-making missionaries, and that they had a goal to raise up many more.[46]

Despite having such an established history, many outside the Philippines still think of the Philippines as a receiving church rather than a sending church because of their relative poverty. We must stop looking at the poor as mere recipients of our aid and see them as partners in the global work God has called us to do together.

If there will be change in a million villages, the truth and transforming power of the gospel will be taken from village to village *by villagers*. National movements will be led by national champions. The rural poor will be *senders* rather than just *receivers*.

---

46 David Lim, Davidlim53's Blog, July 22, 2011, https://davidlim53.wordpress.com/2011/07/.

Embracing a Right View of Ourselves

In the previous section we discussed the need for those who have been blessed financially to see the economically poor as stewards rather than victims, subjects rather than objects, teachers as well as learners, and senders as well as receivers. This new perspective will require humility that involves listening and learning from each other.

Our understanding of the nature and causes of poverty determines how we respond to it. It also colors how we think about "the poor," and how we relate to them. Based on what we believe about poverty, we make assumptions that shape our opinion of others, and our status in relationship to them.

In Romans 12, Paul describes the kind of relationships God intends for his body. He calls us to view other believers as one with us in the body of Christ, and not to consider ourselves more highly than we should (vv. 3-5).

> It is a lack of introspection that often causes the materially rich to be relationally impoverished.

Unfortunately, those who have been blessed financially often see the poor as charity cases who need rescuing rather than as brothers and sisters who have much to give. The financially blessed often see themselves as those who need to do the helping, and not as those in need of being helped. However, if we are to grow to be all God wants us to be, we must recognize we need help. We must enter into a relationship with others in a spirit of humility and with the recognition that they have solutions for the problems we are facing. In light of this, we must work to understand our assumptions about poverty and the poor. It is a lack of introspection that often causes the materially rich to be relationally impoverished.

> We must stop looking at the poor as mere recipients of our aid, and see them as partners in the global work God has called us to do together.

Compared to those we classify as "abject poor," most of us in the "developed world" are materially rich. Yet in my experience, as noted previously, I have found many poor people to be relationally rich. At the same time, I encounter many materially rich people in the "developed world" to be relationally poor. In the developed world, our day-to-day life has become a series of transactions with strangers. We pay landscapers to take care of our yards, grocery stores to provide our food, mechanics to service our cars, and doctors to cure our illnesses. In each transaction we are buyers or sellers, but seldom friends.

Families are scattered, the elderly are moved into eldercare facilities, and we sit in "church" next to strangers. We dream of a successful business and of seeing the world, but we seldom sacrifice our ambitions for the sake of others. We live to get rather than to give. We believe in independence and value self-reliance. In so doing, we lose sight of what is really important in life and label our "poverty" as "success." As a consequence, when we go to serve the materially poor, we blindly take our relational poverty with us.

Understanding Poverty from God's Perspective

In order to begin building healthy relationships between the materially poor and the financially blessed, we must develop a biblical understanding of poverty that rejects some of the materialistic assumptions of our worldview in the West. The way we understand the nature and causes of poverty determines how we respond to it. If we believe poverty is a lack of material possessions, then we give. If poverty is a lack of education, then we teach. If poverty is the result of oppression, then we advocate or revolt. If poverty is because of sin, then we evangelize.

I have embraced a definition of poverty that is rooted in Christian theology and has more to do with relationships and well-being than with wealth and technology. In CHE, we use a definition of poverty which is drawn from the concept of shalom and the story of creation in the Bible.

God created the entire universe and everything in it, including the stars, sun, moon, land formations, seas, plants, and animals. He created a man and a woman in his image and made them stewards of all he had made. There was harmony between God, the man, the woman, and the environment in which they lived. Everyone and everything thrived. God evaluated what he had created and called it good.

In the beginning, at creation, there was perfect harmony between *God, self, others, and the environment.* That harmony was lost when Adam and Eve sinned in the Garden of Eden, and humankind became poor. Poverty, viewed from this perspective, is the loss of harmony in any, or all, of those four areas.

To alleviate poverty, therefore, and to create healthy communities is a process of restoring harmony with our Creator and all he created. This means social, mental, physical, and spiritual well-being. It means food security, clean water, adequate housing, supportive families and friends, safety, education, employment, peace with God, emotional stability, and a clear conscience—to mention but a few.

In CHE training, we refer to poverty as being out of harmony with God, self, others, and the environment. If we understand poverty as being out of harmony in one of the four areas listed above, then we are all poor. We are all out of harmony in some way with God's intentions.

Ironically, the "rich" and the "poor" often mirror each other in their poverty. As Myers, in *Walking with the Poor*, puts it: "Too little food makes us weak and susceptible to disease; too much food makes us overweight and susceptible to heart disease and cancer. The poor have inadequate housing; the non-poor are often slaves to their houses."[47]

Relationships of the poor and the non-poor alike are marred by shame, fear, guilt, bitterness, hostility, and brokenness of every kind. The poor and the non-poor are both alienated from God by sin. The truth is that we all live in networks of relationships that do not work for our well-being. We are all poor. It is essential that we take this perspective with us when we leave home to serve others.

Mutually Transforming Relationships

> To be poor is to be out of harmony with God, self, others, or the environment. Understood in this way, we are all poor.

Armed with a biblical understanding of poverty, we are now ready to think about the kind of relationship God intends between the materially poor and the financially blessed. From the perspective of a materialistic worldview, rather than a biblical worldview, the tendency of the financially blessed is to think they know how to solve the problems of the poor and it is their responsibility to do so. As a consequence, they take control of the processes for the development of the poor and deliver their solutions in the form of projects.

At a task force meeting at the headquarters of MAI, author and missiologist Jim Engel, posed this question to our leaders: "Who runs this organization?" That can be a real question for a nonprofit organization in which donations often come with strings attached. Organizations chasing after funding can quickly become donor-driven by accepting monetary gifts that require them to be responsive to the intentions of the donor rather than to the needs of the people being served.

> If we are to grow to be all God wants us to be, we must recognize that we need the help of others.

In thinking about our work in poor communities, we must ask the same question: "Who runs the organization?" When people with relative wealth come to serve people living in abject poverty, a golden rule often applies. Sadly, it is not the Golden Rule that Jesus taught, but rather: "He who has the gold, rules." The exercising of control by the wealthier party has always been an issue in missions; and while we are finally coming to grips with the effects of colonialism and paternalism, we still need to answer the question of who is truly making the decisions that impact the lives of the economically poor.

---

47 Bryant Myers, *Walking with the Poor: Principles and Practices of Transformational Development* (Maryknoll, NY: Orbis, 1999), 89.

In community work, keeping this potential for a power struggle in mind is central to the effectiveness of any development program. One of our key principles for wholistic ministry in CHE is local ownership and initiative. We have learned from experience that sustainable programs are owned by the people and built on local initiative.

The outsider can bring vision, perspective, and knowledge not otherwise available to the insiders, and progress may be unlikely apart from external input. But the power dynamics between the development worker and the villager must be understood and carefully considered when entering into relationships. Transformation is not what we do for somebody else, but rather what God does when we enter into a mutual relationship of sharing and receiving.

Myers refers to the process of transformation as the coming together of two stories. One story is that of the outsider who approaches a community to facilitate change; the other is that of the insider who lives in a community which could benefit from change. Each has a history, shared knowledge and experience, and a future. Both have a place in the framework of God's larger story. As the outsider comes together to work with the insider, their stories are intertwined for a while; and in their interaction with each other, they are both transformed. Later, when they go their separate ways, it is inevitable that both parties have been changed by what they learned and experienced together.

Approaching a working relationship with this perspective of collaboration, the underlying question changes. It is no longer one of management—Who runs the organization?—but of introspection—What is my attitude in this potentially transforming relationship? Jesus, by commanding his disciples not to exercise authority over others but to be the servant and slave of all, changed the question. He shifted the focus from control to impact, from ruling to serving, from power to humility, and from position to relationship. Jesus called the disciples together and said,

> You know that the rulers of the Gentiles lord it over them, and their high officials exercise authority over them. Not so with you. Instead, whoever wants to become great among you must be your servant, and whoever wants to be first must be your slave—just as the Son of Man did not come to be served, but to serve, and to give his life as a ransom for many. (Matt 20:25–28)

Missionaries, no matter whether abroad or at home, must keep this relational quality of Jesus at the forefront of their minds. They must not go to control, but to contribute; not to rule, but to serve; not with arrogant and ethnocentric attitudes, but with humble, learning hearts; not with savior complexes, but as brothers and sisters in Christ. Rather than going and doing for people, we must enter into an equal relationship of giving and receiving and allow God to change us all in the process. When we make this shift, our mission endeavors will have long-term impact in our own lives as well as in the lives of those we serve.

Respecting the Poor as Made in the Image of God

Sustainable programs are owned by local people and built on local initiative.

Reestablishing honor and dignity are part of God's plan for the restoration of humans to the people they were created to be. The fact that human beings were made in the image and likeness of God automatically endows them with value and worth. This is a powerful truth that gives purpose and protection to every individual regardless of race, gender, or social status.

Jesus commanded his disciples not to exercise authority over others, but to serve. He shifted the focus of our work from control to impact, from ruling to serving, from power to humility, and from position to relationship.

The power of this truth was brought home to me by events in an animistic village in the Pacific. A woman in the village died. The men of the village went to the local medium to determine the cause of death. The medium consulted with the spirits on behalf of the community. After consulting with the spirits, the medium declared that the woman died because four other women from the village had worked sorcery against her. The elders took immediate action and tortured and interrogated the four women, forcing them to confess their "crime." Late one night, with faces painted in pale demonic shades to conceal their identities, several men from the village raided the women's homes to kill them.

I don't know the details of exactly how these women were murdered, although common practices in such situations included beheading, being burned alive, or hanging by wire rope. Three women from the community were killed that night; the fourth woman was set on fire but managed to flee to the road, where she was rescued and eventually found her way to Ruth (not her real name), a CHE trainer and health official working with the community.

I happened to be with Ruth on the day she visited the village with the intention of confronting the situation. The people of the village were gathered under a tree to talk about their progress since the CHE team's last visit. Aware of what happened, Ruth approached the community with the intent of confronting the elders about the murders.

Ruth moved to the center of the circle surrounded by the elders sitting on the ground with their legs crossed and others from the community standing behind them. She initiated the discussion by asking why nothing had been done about the gardens and latrines. They replied, "We were distracted by our problem."

Ruth rose to her feet and looked the men of the village in the eyes. "What you have done is murder," she said. "How dare you turn on your mothers who nursed you? The women you have killed were made in God's image, and you have killed 'God's images.' You will not escape."

The men could only stare at the ground, obviously feeling shame, but showing no sign of genuine remorse and sorrow. The CHE leader demanded that these men recognize it was wrong to kill and that these women had a right to life that is rooted in the fact they were made in the image of God.

Murder is wrong because it is an attack on God's image and a devaluing of the inherent and immeasurable worth (dignity) that comes from being made in the image and likeness of God (Gen 9:6). Abortion is wrong for the same reason. Our behavior toward one another as human beings should respect the dignity and worth of every person. The fact that we are made in God's image gives us certain inalienable rights, including the right to life. Murders, massacres, concentration camps, and abortions are all negative consequences that flow from the rejection or neglect of the truth that humans are made in the image of God.

Being made in God's image not only gives us dignity and worth, but it also defines our role in the world God made (vocation). Humans were placed by God on this earth to have "dominion" over the rest of creation. We were made to be stewards and managers—cultivators of the garden in which God placed us.

An experienced Christian community development worker from the Philippines observed that cleanliness and beautification are often among the first indicators that a community is transforming. That is to say, when members of a community suddenly take an interest in cleanliness and beautification, they may be showing outward signs that they are recovering their inherent vocation as stewards of all that God has given them.

Poverty, then, viewed from this perspective, can be defined as a loss of both dignity and vocation. Those who are economically poor often see themselves as victims of circumstance rather than as stewards of resources. Personal development requires that dignity be restored, and individuals begin to see themselves as of inherent and immeasurable worth because they are made in the image of God. Personal development also requires that people recover their vocation and function in the role for which they were created. Let me illustrate this with a short story.

In a small village in Central Asia, the residents were struggling for survival and at a loss what to do. For six consecutive years, gypsy moths had invaded the land, stripping the trees of their foliage and causing nearly five hundred acres of fruit trees not to produce, but to be completely barren. It had gotten to the point that the men of the village were leaving the area in hopes of finding work in nearby Russia. Their departure left the women to raise their children alone with inadequate resources. Sometimes the men left and never came back. One woman expressed her remorse: "If just six trees would bear fruit, my husband would not have to go to Russia."

Meeting with Village Elders

A CHE team approached the village, wishing to share the good news of the kingdom in both word and deed. An elder in the village admonished the team leader, saying, "Unless you have been sent by God, you cannot solve this problem." The people believed that the plague of the gypsy moths had been sent by God as punishment for their sin. The people in this community saw themselves as persons to be pitied; our volunteer team saw them as people made in the image of God, with the capacity as stewards of the earth to manage and overcome the problem they faced.

> Being made in God's image gives dignity, worth, and the right to life. It also defines our role in the world God made as stewards of creation's resources.

To the people of the community, the plague was much more than an agricultural problem causing some trees to no longer bear fruit. The gypsy moths presented a social problem—families were splitting up. The pests created an economic problem—the people's primary income source was no longer available. The villagers also experienced the plague as a physical problem—without adequate food, energy levels were low. Lastly, the situation was viewed as a spiritual problem—it was believed that the plague of the gypsy moths was a curse from God.

The Christian team gathered the local farmers and facilitated a dialogue about what was happening. The farmers themselves described the behavior and life cycle of the moths. Collectively, they knew quite a bit; in fact, much more than the team from the outside. They had observed that the gypsy moths laid their eggs in sacks in the soil. They also knew that when the eggs hatched, small black-headed caterpillars emerged that would crawl across the ground in the night, climb the trunks to the tops of the trees, and feast on the leaves.

Having identified this cycle, the villagers were encouraged; and together, they came up with a plan to solve the problem. Everyone set out to find and destroy the egg sacks before they hatched. Even the children helped in the hunt. Then, they trapped and killed the caterpillars that weren't killed by tying cloth around the trunks of the trees. When the caterpillars would climb up the trees at night to eat the leaves, they would get caught in the cloth. In the morning, the farmers would go into the orchards and simply smash the destructive insects. An agronomist was also consulted to help them secure and apply the proper pesticide.

I visited this Central Asian village about a year after the CHE team started their work. When I arrived, the local men and women were already celebrating a $60,000 harvest of apricots! Because of their collective efforts, nearly nineteen thousand trees had recovered from the gypsy moth plague and had begun to produce fruit once more. The return in revenue was drawing the men home from Russia; at the last report, more than 323 men had returned to be with their families.

The villagers recognized the transformation that had taken place in their community and were insisting on building a monument to honor the Christian team. The CHE volunteers refused, reminding the people of what they had initially said: "Unless you have been sent by God, you cannot solve this problem." God was revealing himself to them, and the best response was to give him glory for the changes happening in the area.

During my visit, the elders of the community took me to meet the principal of their local school, perhaps because he was one of the few villagers who spoke English. After exchanging formalities, I felt a strong urge to pray. This being a Muslim community, I asked permission to pray in Jesus' name. The principal agreed, so I prayed, "Lord, we thank you for your presence here with us. Thank you for pouring out your blessing on the people of this community and revealing yourself to them. I pray that you will continue to bless them and continue to reveal yourself to them. In Jesus' name, amen."

My prayer was well received. In parting, the principal spoke these words: "There are many stones in our country, but our hearts are not stone. There are many rivers in our country, and our hearts are like rivers flowing with love for you."

Another community member, a woman who had been trained by the Christian team to work with expectant mothers to ensure healthy pregnancies and safe deliveries, tugged at my arm on my way out the door. She looked me in the eye and said with a trembling voice, "Sir, I just want you to know, we serve the same God!"

The members of this community are on the road to recovering their identity as people made in the image of God. They are beginning to see themselves as stewards of creation rather than as victims cursed by God. The walls of hostility between Muslim and Christian neighbors are falling. And the people of the community are willing to learn about Jesus.

In order to return this gift of dignity to the people and communities we serve, we must focus not on what they lack, but rather on who they are and what they can become. We must see their strengths, abilities, and assets. We must focus on their potential rather than their need. We must believe that all are made in the image of God, and therefore treat each one with equal dignity. We must value the relationship with those we are called to serve and recognize it as mutually transforming. We must have confidence in the fact that the other person has as much to offer as we do, and that we will receive from them as much, or more, than we give.

As we consider our areas of ministry, whether abroad or at home, we need to be watchful of the "savior complex" that can hinder our interactions. Short-term mission teams, for example, that have not reflected on this principle of equal dignity often do more harm than good. Instead of recognizing the locals' abilities and assets, the visitors fall into the trap of seeing those whom they go to serve as lacking. Consequently, short-term teams frequently only provide temporary relief for a situation, instead of long-term solutions. In this way, a mindset of poverty is unknowingly reinforced, leaving the members of a community passive and dependent. For long-term, sustainable solutions to be effective, people must be active participants in their own growth and development. We do others a disservice when we focus on what is lacking rather than concentrating on the fact that everyone is made in the image of God.

The lesson from the village for the church worldwide is that there are not two (or more) classes of people in God's economy, but only one. In Matthew 25:34–40, Jesus declared that anyone who serves the poor, serves him; and anyone who refuses the poor, refuses him. In saying this, Jesus addressed not only the entitlements or rights of the poor, but also their worth or dignity. As such, he not only identified himself with the lowly, he simultaneously, associated the lowly with himself as king of all.

This is a first principle for ministry with and among the poor: We must see them not for what they lack, but for who they are. They are made in the image of God, with mind and will capable of participating in choices that affect their lives. They are stewards of creation, with the right to make choices and manage their own futures. They are full members of the family, not strangers or foreigners.

Service in the Context of Relationship

Healthy relationships between the economically poor and the materially blessed will be mutually transforming.

In concluding the section on the dignity of the material poor, and the kind of relationship that God intends between the economically poor and the financially blessed, I need to address the importance of relationship in regard to charitable activities. Many charities sound worthwhile, with names and goals promising cures for cancer, heart disease, and other worthy causes. Most charities are, in fact, honest and put their charitable dollars to good use. However, this is not always the case, and millions of donor dollars are wasted every year.[48]

Not too long ago I joined a group from our church in helping to stock a food pantry. As we sorted the donated goods into boxes, I wondered about the people who would receive this help. There would be many who truly needed the food and would be blessed by the gift. On the other hand, there would also be those who would come and abuse the system. I wondered how those distributing the food

---

48 Matt Viola, "State Charity Reports: How Much Donor Money Is Wasted in Your State?" *Charity Navigator*, March 1, 2009, https://www.charitynavigator.org/index.cfm?bay=content.view&cpid=400.

would determine who should receive it. The question was purely hypothetical. Somebody with more experience than myself would make the decision. But it sparked my thinking.

Systems are guided by well-intentioned policies and regulations that are unbending and undiscerning. Sadly, large charitable organizations are subject to greater abuse because the giving is *not* done in the context of relationship and the majority applying for assistance are total strangers. This makes it tough at times to sort out the needy from the greedy. Are we helping a total stranger through a hard time, or enabling that stranger with bad habits, addictions, or unhealthy dependencies? The answer to this dilemma is giving in the context of relationship. If I am giving to a family member or a friend, then I have a pretty good idea of whether that person has fallen on hard times and truly needs the assistance, or whether they have an unhealthy addiction that would be better addressed in other ways.

Developing Healthy Relationships between North and South

Deborah Ajulu, an African researcher, identifies three kinds of partnerships between the Global North and the Global South: 1) a horse and rider; (2) a cow and milker; and (3) two oxen equally yoked together. The horse and rider portray a situation where the northern "rider" holds the reins and decides the course of action. The cow and milker portray a partnership in which the southern farmer "milks" the north for everything he can get. And the equally yoked oxen represent a partnership in which both partners contribute, receive, and pull together toward the same goals.

The "cow and milker" and the "horse and rider" types of partnerships are birthed by charitable systems that are well-intentioned but often undiscerning. Because the relationship is short-term and distant, it is more prone to abuse than to a true a partnership between people who really know one another and are accountable to each other. As a result, these kinds of partnerships lack accountability and can quickly become codependent. The north enjoys the ride, and the south wants the milk. They manipulate each other for their own ends.

In Ajulu's third scenario, in which the relationship is compared to two oxen equally yoked together, the partners are bound together and each one knows the other. They both have something to give, and they both receive a benefit. Giving takes place in the context of relationship. Together they achieve something that neither of them could do alone. Developing a relationship where North and South are equally yoked together requires that we get to know each other before we start giving.[49]

---

49 Deborah Ajulu, *Holism in Development* (Monrovia, CA: MARC, 1996).

I remember speaking to a group of Americans in Phoenix, Arizona, who were involved either with short-term missions or as members of their church's mission committee. In talking about the North–South partnership, I made the proposition that while Americans tend to begin with projects and work toward relationship, the majority world begins with relationship and works toward projects. This statement seemed to create some dissonance in the minds of my American friends, so I turned to a guest in the room, a pastor from Eastern Europe, and put the question to him. He stood with a flabbergasted look on his face and said with great emotion, "I don't see how you can work together if you don't know each other."

What was at issue was mutuality, a coming together on equal terms to love each other, learn from each other, and achieve something together which neither could do alone. In the chapters that follow, we will explore basic principles that not only provide mutuality, but that strengthen and unite ministries on both sides of the divide for a greater global impact.

CHAPTER 5
Change That God Intends

Recovering the Priorities of Jesus

As followers of Jesus who want to be obedient to everything Jesus commanded, we look carefully at the teaching and ministry of Jesus, seeking to understand his priorities and allowing them to correct and shape ours. Our pursuit of his ideals and perfections is an open-ended process, and we remain constantly attentive to his teaching and example as a corrective to our own.

In the following pages I will share priorities that seem to be dominant themes in the ministry of Jesus, but which were obscured by my own traditions and church culture. Fortunately, in the course of my work overseas, these priorities were called to my attention by people and experiences in my ministry journey.

Some who read this chapter will wonder why I am stating the obvious. Others who come from backgrounds like mine may find that these priorities have been veiled or overshadowed by the church culture in which they were raised.

I am on a transforming journey toward a more transformational ministry. The change always begins with me. Sometimes that change is extremely painful. In spite of the pain, I am grateful to God, who is faithful to his promises and will ultimately complete the work he has begun in me (Phil 1:6).

Acting Justly and Loving Mercy

Some years ago, I was a member of a big church in an area of town that was of high socioeconomic status. It was the kind of church that seats a thousand people in theater type seating, with a large balcony, where the music every week is as good as any concert people might pay to attend. I was sure that when the world looked in the door of my church, they would be entertained by the performances and attracted to the message. And that was not all. Couples' retreats, at $450 for a weekend, were regularly available and in high demand; youth camps were a big hit, and parents didn't seem to think twice about the $600 per child price tag.

The elders were all responsible men living in big homes and driving nice cars. They communicated their vision for saving souls, maintaining better programs, and continuing to build a bigger church. But a question haunted me: With all of these programs, performances, and people, would the world see the values of the kingdom at work?

Jesus came preaching the good news of the kingdom of God. It was a message of forgiveness of sins and eternal life. It was also a message of compassion, justice, reconciliation, and freedom in the present life. It was salvation for the sinner, and good news to the poor and the oppressed. The message of the kingdom had implications for the present and the future.

> **The Old Testament passage that Jesus chose to describe his mission makes it clear that the hurting, the poor, and the oppressed would be the focus of his ministry.**

Jesus spoke directly on a number of occasions about why he came and what he came to do. He said he came to do the will of the Father (John 6:38), to bring light into the darkness (John 12:46), to seek and to save what was lost (Luke 19:10), and to give his life as a ransom for many (Matt 20:28). He came preaching repentance, offering the kingdom of God (Mark 1:15, 38; John 18:37) and life to the full (John 10:10).

In his inaugural address at the beginning of his ministry, however, Jesus encapsulated his mission and the purpose for his coming. He went to the synagogue in the community where he grew up, opened a scroll, and read from the book of Isaiah:

> The Spirit of the Lord is on me, because he has anointed me to preach good news to the poor. He has sent me to proclaim freedom for the prisoners and recovery of sight for the blind, to release the oppressed, to proclaim the year of the Lord's favor. Then he rolled up the scroll, gave it back to the attendant and sat down. The eyes of everyone in the synagogue were fastened on him, and he began by saying to them, "Today this scripture is fulfilled in your hearing." (Luke 4:18–21)

On that day, Jesus declared himself to be the anointed one of whom the prophet spoke, and he appropriated the words of Isaiah as his own personal mission statement. He used these words to explain to the people in his hometown who he was and why he came.

The passage Jesus chose to describe his mission made it clear that the hurting, the poor, and the oppressed would be a focal point of his ministry. Jesus would take those who had been pushed to the periphery—the suffering, the alienated, and the marginalized—and move them to the center. The last would be first.

Putting the Last First

Near the end of his public ministry, Jesus described a day when he would sit on his throne as judge and separate the righteous from the unrighteous based on how they responded to the needs of the poor. On that day, he will say to the righteous:

"I was hungry and you gave me something to eat, I was thirsty and you gave me something to drink, I was a stranger and you invited me in, I needed clothes and you clothed me, I was sick and you looked after me, I was in prison and you came to visit me....I tell you the truth, whatever you did for one of the least of these brothers of mine, you did for me" (Matt 25:35–36, 40).

Jesus puts himself in the place of the poor and marginalized and accepts service that is offered to them as if it were offered to him. Even more than accepting this service, he separates the righteous from the unrighteous based upon it. Acts of service to the poor are acts of righteousness received by the King himself. They are not only good deeds that help the hurting, but genuine acts of worship that bring honor to Jesus. As Christ's followers, action on behalf of the poor should characterize our lives and ministries. Jesus identifies himself as brother to the hungry, the thirsty, the stranger, the naked, the sick, and the prisoner. The righteous serve them; the unrighteous do not.

Jesus also promises to reward those who serve the poor and marginalized. They will hear him say: "Come, you who are blessed by my Father; take your inheritance, the kingdom prepared for you since the creation of the world" (Matt 25:34).

Like the poor, the sick, and the prisoner, children were among the most vulnerable in ancient Rome, and Jesus identified himself with them as well. Roman fathers had the right, without punishment, to get rid of a child, sell a child into slavery, or even kill a child. Some children would be sold into a life of prostitution. Some men even exercised their paternal right to practice "exposure," in which their children were taken from the house by a slave, who then left them somewhere unknown—typically by the roadside or on a heap of garbage—to die or to be picked up by strangers.[50]

The Gospels tell of a time when people were bringing little children to Jesus and the disciples felt the need to intervene and stop these parents. Apparently, children were not at the top of the disciples' scale of priorities for ministry, so they sought to censor and stop what was happening. The disciples' actions reflected a low view of the value of children. This annoyed Jesus, as he recognized that these parents were bringing their young to him as an act of dedication and to receive his blessing upon their futures (Mark 10:13–16).

Jesus reprimanded his disciples for turning away the little children. They shouldn't have been surprised by his response, though. Not long before, the disciples had been arguing over who would be greatest in the kingdom, and Jesus had to intervene. He explained, "If anyone wants to be first, he must be the very

---

50 W. V. Harris, "Child-Exposure in the Roman Empire," Journal of Roman Studies 84 (November 1994): 1–22, https://www.cambridge.org/core/journals/journal-of-roman-studies/article/childexposure-in-the-roman-empire/3410A0618E4B37F1CF1EE52B11DC89F4.

last, and the servant of all" (Mark 9:35). Then, to illustrate what he meant, Jesus put a little child in their midst and said, "Whoever welcomes one of these little children in my name welcomes me; and whoever welcomes me does not welcome me but the one who sent me" (Mark 9:37).

Jesus uses the same language to describe his relationship to children that he uses of the hungry, the thirsty, the stranger, the naked, the sick, and the prisoner. Jesus put himself in the place of the children, whom the disciples were turning away, and demanded that his followers welcome and serve them. By making a child the symbol of the one to whom service is rendered, Jesus teaches that service is to be given to those with *less* power in society, not to those with more. Those who are the greatest are the ones who serve the least. Jesus calls us into their service.

This principle was brought home to me one day on a site visit to a CHE ministry in Uganda. Our CHE coordinators in Uganda were Dr. Chris Palacas and his wife, Jane. Chris is a medical doctor serving as a bishop in the Anglican Church of Uganda and Canon to the Archbishop. As Ugandans caught a vision for CHE, Chris and Jane, together with the Church of Uganda, have catalyzed a transformational movement that has impacted more than six hundred communities.

We drove to a small village in Kawala parish, in the Mbale Diocese of Eastern Uganda. As we pulled into the community in our Nissan four-wheel drive truck, people of all ages lined the streets, singing and dancing their welcome. We got out of the truck and walked in procession into the church building where we were escorted to our seats in front of the gathering crowd. To our right were religious and political dignitaries from all over the district. To our left were the people Chris and Jane had trained—development committee members and community health volunteers. Directly in front of us, in a place of honor surrounded by the community, were fifty-three children.

Each one of these fifty-three children—all of them AIDS orphans—had their own story to tell. Some had to drop out of school to take care of their dying parents. Many struggled to find ways to support the family, assuming the role of both caregiver and breadwinner. All were traumatized by grief and loss, compounded for many by the experience of watching their parents die a slow and horrific death. Many felt the stigma and shame associated with AIDS.

The situation in many African villages at this time was desperate, and it was likely to get worse. There were funerals every week. Children were being absorbed into extended families, but the extent of the AIDS problem was pushing the extended family system to the breaking point. With half of all households living in extreme poverty and wage earners being lost to the AIDS pandemic, the strain of caring for extra children can be a burden almost too heavy to bear. Some of the children sitting in front of us were being cared for by aging grandparents, others by older siblings, and still others by aunts and uncles.

The plight of these orphaned children whose parents had died of AIDS, however, had not gone unnoticed as the CHEs in this village began visiting in homes. In response to what they saw, they decided that some action needed to be taken. The volunteer health workers called all the AIDS orphans in the village to come to a meeting on a Tuesday night. At this meeting each child was presented with the scholastic materials (pens and books) they needed in order to attend school. The volunteers gave generously out of their own poverty to provide for the needs of these children. They gave willingly, entirely on their own, without prompting from anyone.

The local CHEs were committed to these children—this was not a one-time charity event. Every Tuesday evening, the orphans were met with love. The community health volunteers continued to care for "the least of these" by feeding them a meal, teaching them God's Word, singing, and praying. Feelings of hopelessness and despair because of such difficult circumstances and at such young ages began to subside. Some of these children come from Muslim homes, and a good number of them have come to Christ.

Had these children been in some other village, they would likely have been neglected, abused, or abandoned. Many AIDS orphans drop out of school, suffer malnutrition, receive little, if any medical care, and experience emotional problems due to unresolved grief. They are more likely to be forced to work long hours, suffer from beatings, and be subject to sexual abuse. Here they were loved, embraced by the community, and given a place of honor.

UNICEF reports that "as of 2019, roughly 13.8 million children under the age of 18 had lost one or both parents to AIDS-related causes. Millions more have been affected by the epidemic, through a heightened risk of poverty, homelessness, school dropout, discrimination and loss of opportunities.... In 2019, sub-Saharan Africa accounted for approximately 68 percent of people of all ages living with HIV and 88 percent of children and adolescents living with HIV worldwide."[51] These children do not need orphanages, they need families. Communities must take ownership of the problem and accept the responsibility of caring for their own orphans. Villages like the one in Kawala parish, Uganda, are leading the way, modeling what must be done to care for these growing numbers of children with neither father nor mother.

As Chris, Jane, and I prepared to get back into our truck and head back to the city, I found myself surrounded by a sea of children singing, "If you're happy and you know it, say amen!"

> In this remote Ugandan village, little ones who in other places would have been stigmatized, neglected, abused, or abandoned, were given a place of honor. This is as it should be among the people of God.

---

51 "Global and Regional Trends," UNICEF, July, 2020, https://data.unicef.org/topic/hivaids/protection-care-and-support-for-children-affected-by-hiv-and-aids/.

I stood in the center of their celebration, spinning as they held my hands and danced in circles around me. The smiles on their faces brought tears to my eyes. They well up again now as I think about it.

In this remote Ugandan village, little ones who in other places would have been stigmatized, neglected, abused, or abandoned, were given a place of honor at the table. This is as it should be among the people of God.

Restoring Dignity to Broken People

Salvation is a gift from God. In saving us from sin, God not only removes our guilt and releases us from condemnation, but he also cleanses us of our shame and restores us to a place of honor (Rom 9:33; 10:11). In our Western way of thinking, we tend to focus primarily on the freedom from guilt and condemnation. In contrast, salvation—in more relational cultures—is the restoration of a broken relationship, with an emphasis on the reparation of those things separate us from a loving Father and a place of dignity and honor. We would do well to remember each of these elements, as they are all, together, a constant theme in Scripture.

> **In saving us from sin, God not only removes our guilt and releases us from condemnation, but he also cleanses us from shame and restores us to a place of honor.**

In Isaiah 54, God speaks to a broken and scattered nation and promises to remove their shame and restore them to a place of dignity and honor:

> Do not be afraid; you will not be put to shame. Do not fear disgrace; you will not be humiliated. You will forget the shame of your youth and remember no more the reproach of your widowhood. For your Maker is your husband—the LORD Almighty is his name—the Holy One of Israel is your Redeemer; he is called the God of all the earth. (Isa 54:4–5)

In the New Testament, God says similar things about believers: "You are a chosen race, a royal priesthood, a holy nation, God's own people, in order that you may proclaim the mighty acts of him who called you out of darkness into his marvelous light. Once you were not a people, but now you are God's people" (1 Pet 2:9–10 NRSV).

God is not only saving us from condemnation, but he is also restoring us to a place of honor and dignity. If our ministries will reflect the fullness of the salvation which Jesus offers, then we must proclaim a salvation through repentance and faith in Christ that both saves from condemnation and restores broken relationships recovering the dignity and honor that was lost in the fall.

Restoring dignity to the outcast was a major theme in Jesus' ministry. From the very outset of his public life, Jesus made it clear he intended to restore dignity to the poor, to prisoners, to the blind, and to the oppressed.

We find a beautiful illustration of restoring dignity in the parable Jesus told about the prodigal son in Luke 15. When the prodigal returned home after squandering his father's wealth in a distant land, the father took actions that not only released him from punishment but restored him to a place of honor. He arrayed him in his "best robe," and put a ring on the young man's finger, both symbols of sonship and authority (Isa 61:10; Eph 1:5). He received him back as a son rather than a servant.

Jesus used this parable to illustrate the salvation he offers to all who will believe. God not only saves us from punishment, but he restores us to a place of respect and privilege where it has been lost. The point of this story is that God restores broken sinners to a place of dignity and honor, and that we should not only celebrate this but should participate with him in the process of that restoration.

This raises a number of questions for our own introspection: Are we deliberate about restoring dignity to the poor? Do we run to meet the poor and broken, giving dignity and honor where it has been lost? Do we give honor to those in our fellowship who are plastered with stigmas because of brokenness, poverty, disability, illness, or a criminal record? Do we focus our ministries on those who are "whole," or are we deliberate about engaging those on the margins?

James addresses this problem in the early church. When preference was given to the rich, James intervenes by affirming the dignity of the poor and asking the question: "Has not God chosen those who are poor in the eyes of the world to be rich in faith and to inherit the kingdom he promised those who love him?" He then goes on to insist that believers must not show favoritism and thereby dishonor the poor (James 2:1–9).

If we want our ministries to reflect the priorities of Jesus, then we must aim to restore dignity and honor where it has been lost. This truth has enormous social implications. The church, called to restore dignity and honor, breaks down the barriers between rich and poor and between elites and common citizens. The church unites the races and brings people together from every tribe and nation. The church looks after the needs of the poor, the outcast, and the immigrant. The church rejects discrimination based on gender and race. The church teaches love for enemies and is a friend of sinners.

Doing Good Works That Glorify God

In the early 1990s, I visited a CHE team working in the city of Ozamiz, on the northern part of the island of Mindanao, Philippines, in an area populated by both Muslims and Christians. Sometime before I arrived, Ozamiz conducted an operation aimed at gathering and treating individuals living on the streets with mental illnesses. One case was particularly acute. A woman was found lying on a sidewalk, curled up in the fetal position. She was unable to walk or even to speak, and her skin was covered with feces, sores, and scabs. She smelled so bad that government officials used a fishing net to pick her up off the street and take her to the hospital. When she arrived at the hospital, the doctors refused to treat her, and told the officials to take her back to the street where she belonged.

Pastor Greg Subrabas served as pastor of Diguan Bible Baptist Church, a small congregation located in a village outside the city. He learned of what happened and went to find the woman. He picked her up off the street and carried her to his church. His wife, Zenaida, bathed the woman, washing away the feces and dirt and cleaning her wounds. Then the two of them began to work with the woman, coaching her through a regimen of physical therapy exercises. Pastor Greg placed her in a chair with a coconut husk under one foot and started moving the foot and husk in a circular motion, as Filipinos do when they wax their floors. After she polished for a while with her right foot, Greg moved the husk was to the woman's left foot and helped her repeat the motion. After some weeks her feet and legs grew stronger and she began to walk and talk again.

Word got out throughout the province that God had healed her, and Diguan Bible Baptist Church started to be known as a place where people could go if they needed help. Battered wives, orphaned children, epileptics, the mentally insane, people with tuberculosis and every other imaginable dreaded disease—all were welcomed, and Greg didn't turn any away.

The church building itself is a simple structure, with a cement floor and a corrugated tin roof. As abandoned and helpless people came for refuge and healing, Pastor Greg added small rooms to accommodate them to the side of the chapel. On my visit, he walked me through a maze of primitive rooms, made with temporary materials, built off the side of the chapel and housing all kinds of hurting people. Standing at the front of the chapel near the pulpit, I looked down the center aisle past the plastic chairs lined up in rows and saw what looked like a prison cell at the back of the room. The room had cement walls, bars in the glassless windows, and a single door on the side. I asked Greg about it, and he replied, "This is where people who are out of control stay. Sometimes when they come here, they are completely out of control. We have no choice but to put them in this isolated room and pray for them until they calm down." He went on to say, "God has his timing for each one of them—sometimes it's weeks, sometimes it's months."

As Greg talked about all that was happening, I noticed he would always refer to those who stayed in the church as "my family." It didn't matter that he had no regular income or means of supporting the many coming for help. In fact, he wore a dirty T-shirt, a visibly old pair of pants, and cheap rubber slippers. Nevertheless, all who arrived at the church were welcome. I asked Greg how he supported them all. "We get up early in the morning and pray for our breakfast.

After breakfast, we start praying for our lunch." Greg added, "There are sixty souls in this house, all living by faith."

Greg then took me on a tour of the facility. In one of the add-on bamboo-framed rooms, he introduced me to two individuals I could hardly stand to look at. They both had only recently been

> True Christian ministry aims to restore dignity and honor and break down barriers between rich and poor, men and women, races and ethnicities. The church unites races, tribes, and nations as one body in Christ.

brought to the church. One of them, many years previously, had been a promising young student, studying to be a lawyer at a prestigious university in Manila. Just before his graduation, he joined an activist group and was thrown into prison by the Marcos regime. By the time he was released from prison, he was starving and insane. The other man was found on the street. He was so malnourished that he was literally skin and bones. His thighs were no bigger around than my forearms, and his skin was black and spotted with sores. Greg said that when this man arrived, his whole body oozed blood and pus. Greg took the time to carefully scrub off the crust on his skin and clean his sores.

Greg called on the CHE team in Ozamiz, including Leo and Mary Tago, for additional help. Leo was a dentist, and his wife, Mary, served as a family practice physician; they volunteered time in service to Pastor Greg's "family." Mary treated the two men who had recently arrived for malnutrition, scabies, infection, and, in the case of one of the gentlemen, diabetes. They were on their way to recovery, but still had a long, long way to go. Greg and his team were committed for the long haul and were looking forward to the day when these men would witness a complete healing in mind, heart, and body by the power of the gospel and the love of Christ's followers.

Back in the chapel, with children running around me, I was introduced to a healthy-looking man in his late twenties. Surprisingly, he had been a drug addict and alcoholic for ten years before he was brought to the church. The government had given up their efforts at rehabilitation, saying he was incurable. "They couldn't have been more mistaken," Greg said, "for with God all things are possible!" The man showed me a picture of himself as a drug addict—the contrast was striking. Then he told me, "I want to go back to my barangay (village) and preach Christ to them." He praised the Lord and gave God the credit for healing him.

Still in the chapel, I met yet another woman from the church. She had three noticeable scars—permanent marks left by gashes made with some kind of sharp object: a scar on each of her cheeks and a third mark on her forehead. The woman had been a battered wife, but now she, along with her husband and children, were living at the church and ministering to other battered women who came to the church for help.

She testified, "Look at my face. My husband did this to me, and I forgave him. If God can forgive us, then we can forgive those who sin against us." This woman, like so many others in the "family," had seen Greg's good works, given her heart to Christ, and by her spontaneous and unstoppable witness was giving glory to our Father in heaven.

Diguan Bible Baptist Church ministers to those who have been discarded by society and rejected by the medical community as hopeless cases. A good percentage of the individuals who come to the church are eventually rehabilitated, not with medicine or pills, but with the love of Jesus. Many remain at the church as staff to minister to other residents and to members of the community, who arrive almost daily. The church has become a dumping ground for people discarded by society as unbearable. At Diguan, people find love, acceptance, and hope.

Because Ozamiz sits on the border between a Muslim and a Christian area, devotees used to gather in the marketplace to debate. Catholics, Muslims, Protestants, and Iglesia Ni Kristo (which means "Church of Christ," and is a nontrinitarian sect that began in the Philippines) adherents were all represented. In the middle of one debate, a Muslim man stood to his feet and said, "You all are debating the real church. I know the real church. It is in Diguan!"

It was not the debates that led this Muslim man to recognize the truth and make such a declaration, but the good works done by the church. If as a church we focus on evangelism and neglect social action, we shouldn't be surprised when those around us of different faiths, or no faith at all, fail to hear the message we proclaim. As Jesus said, when our light shines and others see our good works, they will glorify our Father in heaven (Matt 5:16).

Evangelism in the Context of Love and Good Works

Many evangelicals view evangelism as a completely rational process. Believers make truth claims. Hearers consider those truth claims and make a decision to either believe or reject them. Working from that assumption, the command to make disciples is a command to teach and preach the truth.

As I have illustrated in the previous section, however, evangelism is often most effective in the context of love and good works. We certainly see this in the life of Jesus, who healed the sick, caused the blind to see, and cleansed lepers. He condemned prejudice and racism, commanding his followers to love and serve Samaritans. He redeemed prostitutes and traitorous tax collectors, cleansed the temple, and loved his enemies.

Jonah Lehrer, in his book *How We Decide*, argues from neuroscience that the decisions we make are a blend of both feeling and reason. He concludes that it isn't just facts that influence our thinking, but relationships and emotion as well. In an interview, Lehrer said,

"For the first time in human history, we can look inside our minds and see how we actually think. It turns out that we weren't designed to be rational or logical or even particularly deliberate. Instead, our mind holds a messy network of different areas, many of which are involved with the production of emotion. Whenever we make a decision, the brain is awash in feeling, driven by its inexplicable passions. Even when we try to be reasonable and restrained, these emotional impulses secretly influence our judgment."[52]

In a similar vein, John Pijanowski, a researcher at the University of Arkansas, identified eight stages of decision-making. He describes the first stage as establishing community as accomplished through the process of creating and nurturing relationships, norms, and procedures that will influence how problems are understood and communicated. According to Pijanowski's research, this happens prior to, or in the midst of, a moral dilemma. In other words, the first stage of the decision-making process is not intellectual, but relational. In establishing community, we choose who we will trust and what assumptions we will bring to the table.[53]

> Perhaps our most convincing argument for the Christian faith is the quality of our relationships rather than the logic of our propositions.

My intention here is not to delve into psychology or neuroscience, but to raise this question: Is evangelism an entirely rational process of making truth claims, or is there more to it than that? In addition to saying that people will see our good works and glorify our Father in heaven, Jesus also said, "By this all men will know that you are my disciples, if you love one another" (John 13:35). Perhaps our most convincing argument is the quality of our relationships rather than the logic of our propositions. Likewise, maybe our actions, so often speaking louder than words, are the most convincing argument for faith in Christ.

Let's consider the dramatic story in Acts 16 about a man who made a decision to follow Christ as a result of the Apostle Paul's outreach in the city of Philippi. We can learn much from his conversion about the process of evangelism. Paul and Silas were going to the local place of prayer when they were met by a demon-possessed slave girl who had the ability to predict the future. She earned a lot of money for her owners by her fortune-telling. The girl followed Paul and his team for many days shouting, "These men are servants of the Most High God, who are telling you the way to be saved" (v. 17). "Finally," Luke writes, "Paul became so troubled that he turned around and said to the spirit, 'In the name of Jesus Christ I command you to come out of her!' At that moment the spirit left her" (v. 18).

---

52 Jonah Lehrer, *How We Decide* (New York: Houghton Mifflin Harcourt, 2009).
53 John Pijanowski, *Eight Stages of Decision Making* (Fayetteville, AR: University of Arkansas, 2009), 7.

When the slave girl's owners realized their source of income from her fortune-telling had been lost because she could no longer tell the future, they dragged Paul and Silas into the marketplace before the magistrates and accused them: "These men are Jews, and are throwing our city into an uproar by advocating customs unlawful for us Romans to accept" (vv. 21–22).

The crowd joined in the attack, and the magistrates had Paul and Silas stripped, severely beaten, and thrown into prison. The jailer was commanded to guard them carefully, so he put them in the inner cell and fastened their feet in stocks.

About midnight Paul and Silas were praying and singing hymns to God, and the other prisoners in the jail were listening. Suddenly there was a violent earthquake that shook the foundations of the prison. The prison doors flew open, and everyone's chains came loose.

The jailer woke up, and when he saw the prison doors open, he drew his sword to kill himself because he thought the prisoners had escaped. Paul saw what was happening and shouted, "Don't harm yourself! We are all here!" The jailer called for lights, rushed inside, and fell trembling before Paul and Silas. He then took them outside and asked, "Sirs, what must I do to be saved?" (vv. 25–30).

"They replied, 'Believe in the Lord Jesus, and you will be saved—you and your household.' Then they spoke the word of the Lord to him and to all the others in his house (vv. 31–32). The jailer then washed the wounds Paul and Silas sustained when they were flogged and beaten; and afterward he and his family were baptized (v. 33).

What was it in this story that brought the jailer to faith in Christ? Was it the preaching of Paul and Silas in the streets of Philippi? Was it the earthquake in the middle of the night? Perhaps it was the fact that Paul and Silas were willing to exchange their freedom for the jailer's life? Or could it be when the apostles spoke the word of the Lord to him and his family?

If I were Paul or Silas, I'm sure I would have taken the earthquake as a sign from God that he wanted me out of there. I would have put on my running shoes and high-tailed it to safety! Instead, Paul and Silas recognized the danger the jailer was in and made a choice to stay in the hard place. They said, in effect, "My life for yours."

Immediately after this exchange, the jailer ran and fell before Paul and Silas and asked them, "What must I do to be saved?" I don't believe it was any one of these things alone that brought salvation to the jailer, but a combination of all of them.

Pastor Fred Gabriel, a CHE coordinator in the Philippines when I served as director there, wrote to me one day about one of his trainers, Beth, who led a woman to the Lord. The moving story Fred told is another example of evangelism in the context of love and good works.

Beth was recovering in the charity ward of the hospital just two days after her operation for breast cancer. A woman with a ruptured ulcer leading to a deadly infection of the abdominal cavity, called peritonitis, was placed in the bed beside her. The doctors knew that if this woman didn't have surgery immediately, she would die. Her family was very poor and had only managed to scrape together about one hundred pesos (two dollars) for her care. That wasn't enough to pay for the medicine she needed for even one day. Since the woman and her family would be unable to pay, the doctor refused to do the surgery.

As a concerned Christian, Beth tried to comfort the family, assuring them that God is good, that he is in control, and that he has a plan. After Beth shared the gospel with the family, four of them, including the woman with the ruptured ulcer, prayed to receive Christ. Not very wealthy herself, Beth considered the little bit of money in her possession—money that her friends had donated for her own medical needs. Thinking not just of herself, but also the needs of others, Beth gave some of that money to the woman in the next bed. She then prevailed upon the doctor to perform the surgery.

The doctor agreed, and the woman recovered. She gave thanks to the Lord for saving her, both physically and spiritually. Beth says, "Praise the Lord for the great joy I had in my heart that, in spite of my situation, the Lord is still using me for his glory."

I believe these are the kind of witnesses we ought to be: people who are willing to make the exchange, my life for yours. We need to be people who are genuinely concerned for the needs of others and acting sacrificially to meet those needs. We are called to be people who proclaim the truth of the gospel boldly in the context of love and good works.

Transforming Cultures and Communities

As we consider the subject of transforming communities, we enter territory that has been a source of debate among theologians for centuries. Without a doubt, Jesus is Savior and Lord. He gave his life on the cross in payment for our sins, and he offers forgiveness of sins and new life to all who will believe. He will come again to reign in righteousness and to restore all that was broken by the fall. There is salvation in no other person or path.

Although Jesus is the Savior, he was not an armed revolutionary. His *teaching* was revolutionary, and it changed the course of history. But Jesus, himself, did not take up arms against the government. His revolution would be a revolution of the heart, changing individuals one at a time and culminating in renewed relationships, right values, and changed behaviors.

Was Jesus a reformer? That is a more difficult question. He certainly put pressure on corrupt leaders who oppressed his people; and he stood up for women and the poor, calling them to take part in his ministry. He confronted the love of money and racism. He did all of this while conveying his message of repentance, faith, regeneration, and reconciliation. In fact, it could be argued that it was the pressure he put on political and religious leaders that led to his crucifixion.

Jesus' message had both social and political implications. Salvation and reform were not competing or contradictory ideas in the life and ministry of Jesus; rather they were both elements of his life and of his work. We see Jesus calling individuals to repent and follow him, including a time when he drove the money changers out of the temple in Jerusalem.

The temple was the heart of Jewish society—the center of both religious and political power. The cleansing of the temple was followed by many miracles (see John 2) and would have been headline news in Jerusalem. Those gathered for Passover in that city would have carried the news of the events back home with them, making Jesus the talk of the nation. By overturning the tables of the money changers and driving the merchants out of the temple, Jesus was exposing corruption at the highest levels—and in so doing, calling the nation to repent. This cleansing of the temple by the coming Messiah was predicted by the prophet Malachi more than four hundred years earlier:

> "See, I will send my messenger, who will prepare the way before me. Then suddenly the Lord you are seeking will come to his temple; the messenger of the covenant, whom you desire, will come," says the Lord Almighty.
>
> But who can endure the day of his coming? Who can stand when he appears? For he will be like a refiner's fire or a launderer's soap. He will sit as a refiner and purifier of silver; he will purify the Levites and refine them like gold and silver. Then the Lord will have men who will bring offerings in righteousness, and the offerings of Judah and Jerusalem will be acceptable to the Lord, as in the days gone by, as in former years.
>
> "So I will come near to you for judgment. I will be quick to testify against sorcerers, adulterers and perjurers, against those who defraud laborers of their wages, who oppress the widows and the fatherless, and deprive aliens of justice, but do not fear me," says the Lord Almighty. (Mal 3:1–5)

Jesus was both Savior and Reformer. He is still that today. He still intends to save us from our sin and transform our lives from the inside out, so that his values are integrated in our relationships, families, and communities. If we are truly followers of Jesus, then we must not separate evangelism from social action, righteousness from justice, faith from repentance, concern for the salvation of souls from concern for those who suffer. We must minister wholistically.

I am an eyewitness to the fact that the change God works in individuals who repent and believe can transform the communities in which they live. One such place is the small town of Bingawan on the island of Panay in the Philippines.

> Jesus is both Savior and Reformer. He saves us from sin and transforms our lives so that the values of his kingdom are reflected in our families and communities.

As I drove toward the village, a number of signs were posted along the dirt road. For example: "This way to Bingawan, but Jesus is the only way to heaven," and "The only leader worth following is the one who is following Christ." As I neared the entrance to the community, I saw another sign that read "Welcome to Bingawan, a Christian Community."

One of the first things I observed when I arrived was that every home in Bingawan had a trash can somewhere in the front yard. This prompted me to look for litter as I drove around town; the only thing I could spot was a single blue drinking straw. Instead of trash, maintained trees and bushes lined the roads. While it could be noted that these roads were still unpaved, this was simply due to the mayor's refusal to pay the bribes demanded by the government for such luxuries.

I wouldn't have believed such a place existed if I hadn't seen it. I have traveled all over the Philippines and have never seen a town like this. For three consecutive years, the national government named Bingawan the cleanest and greenest town in the province. Other towns in the province asked Bingawan to drop out of the competition so one of them could win! In addition to winning the provincial competitions, Bingawan was consistently one of the top ten cleanest and greenest towns in the whole country. The mayor, Safiro Palabrica, was chosen by his peers as the most outstanding mayor in the country for three consecutive terms.

Mayor Palabrica is a committed Christian. He spoke briefly to the group gathered to welcome us, and graciously attributed much of the town's success to the work of the CHE team. Everyone in the room testified to the transformation taking place in their lives and community. One obviously poor woman testified that although she is at the bottom of the socioeconomic scale, she is no longer ashamed to associate with the "big shots," because they have accepted her.

Before I arrived in the community, CHE workers told me that gambling rings had been shut down and crime rates were significantly lower than anywhere else in the country. They also told me there was a jail, and police to guard it, but no prisoners. It sounded too good to be true. I asked Mayor Palabrica if I could see if for myself.

When we arrived at the jail, two guards were waiting for us. They opened the door, and I looked inside. There was a small table with a flower vase in the middle, and a Bible on both sides of the vase. There was a television in one corner. One of the guards quipped, "We even put a television in here, but we can't get anybody to use it!"

I asked Mayor Palabrica if it was true that they never had prisoners. He said occasionally someone will get drunk and cause a little trouble. When that happens, the mayor simply escorts the person to the jail, gives him the keys, and tells him to let himself out when he has become sober.

I was still skeptical. We went back to the municipal hall, where I struck up a conversation with a random individual visiting the mayor's office. In the course of our conversation, the man told me that he was an attorney, but that he and his family had to move away from Bingawan because there was nothing in the town for him to litigate. I was convinced. The changes taking place in this small municipality were real and deep—and they were birthed by the influence of Christian people with a passion for wholistic ministry.

Just as when Jesus tossed the money changers out of the temple, Mayor Palabrica and his CHE-trained staff understood that their faith had social consequences. Love required them to take an active role as reformers as well as evangelists, promoting what is in the best interest of the community for the glory of God. Their work led to a revival in the town of Bingawan that was evidenced by the disappearance of gambling rings, a reduction of crime, a decrease in illness and disease, a rise in agricultural productivity, healthier children, and cleaner streets.

The story of Bingawan captured national attention, bringing honor and glory to the name of Christ. This entire town was changed by the transforming power of the gospel.

> **We are called to be people who proclaim the gospel in the context of love and good works.**

The work done in this town would be repeated in other places around the Philippines and eventually throughout Southeast Asia. The next chapter is a summary of the principles and practices that not only enabled community transformation but contributed to the spread of these successes from community to community.

CHAPTER 6

Change That Multiplies

The Fundamentals of Transformational Movements

In the first part of this book, we discussed some of the priorities of kingdom work as reflected in the ministry and teaching of Jesus that for me, and for others who share my perspective, needed focus and attention. In this chapter, we will explore five principles that are key to wholistic transformational ministry and movements.

I am not the first to advocate principles for service to the poor that lead to transformative outcomes in the lives of those being served. Recent works that make a significant contribution to this discussion include Robert Reese, *Roots and Remedies of the Dependency Syndrome in World Missions*;[54] Bryant Myers, *Walking with the Poor*;[55] Steve Corbett and Brian Fikkert, *When Helping Hurts*;[56] and Robert Lupton, *Toxic Charity* and *Charity Detox*.[57]

Nevertheless, I hope to advance the discussion, drawing from experiences God has given me, by articulating five simple principles which have not only enabled CHE teams around the world to help without hurting, but have empowered them to set off transformational movements that change life for an ever-increasing number of people and communities for generations to come. While I will illustrate these principles with stories from CHE work in villages around the world, each one is applicable to any church that desires to see the lives of individuals and communities transformed, whether in a church, village, town, city, state, or nation. The five principles of wholistic transformational ministry are (1) integration; (2) asset-based development; (3) local ownership; (4) multiplication; and (5) participatory learning. We will examine each one in turn.

> This chapter will unpack five principles that have empowered CHE teams to set off transformational movements in villages around the world.

---

54 Robert Reese, *Roots and Remedies of the Dependency Syndrome in World Missions* (Pasadena, CA: William Carey Library, 2010).

55 Bryant L. Myers, *Walking with the Poor: Principles and Practices of Transformational Development*, rev. ed. (Maryknoll, NY: Orbis, 2011).

56 Steve Corbett and Brian Fikkert, *When Helping Hurts* (Chicago: Moody, 2009).

57 Robert Lupton, *Toxic Charity: How Churches and Charities Hurt Those They Help (And How to Reverse It)* (New York: HarperCollins, 2011); *Charity Detox: What Charity Would Look Like if We Cared about Results* (New York: HarperCollins, 2015).

Transformational Development
Lives and communities transformed by the love of Christ.

Water towers come in many shapes and sizes; however, they need strong legs and a solid foundation on which to stand. So it is with Transformational Development Programs.

LOCAL OWNERSHIP
- Give people with a vision what **they can do** to improve the quality of their lives and minister to others' needs.
- Involve people in identifying needs and resources, and making plans.
- Build cooperation; get people working together.
- Don't blueprint plans from the outside

MULTIPLICATION
- Focus on use of local resources.
- Avoid dependency on outsiders.
- Look beyond sustainability to multiplication.

INTEGRATION
- Keep faith and works together.
- Promote complete obedience to all Jesus commanded.
- Promote development in wisdom, stature, and favor with God and man.

DEVELOPMENT
- Involve people as responsible participants rather than passive recipients.
- Build capacity rather than create dependency.
- Help people to do for themselves rather than doing things for them.

- Cast VISION rather than blueprinting action plans.
- Pose PROBLEMS rather than solutions.
- DIALOGUE rather than lecture.

PARTICIPATORY LEARNING

TRUTH

Principle 1: Integrating the Physical and the Spiritual

The first principle of transformational ministry is integration. Jesus, who commanded us to preach the forgiveness of sins, also commanded us to love our neighbors. More often than not, though,

> As followers of Christ, we don't choose which of his commands is most important, but we choose to obey everything he commanded.

we have focused on just one or the other of these mandates. As followers of Christ, we don't choose which of his commands is most important, but rather we choose to obey everything Jesus commanded. That means caring for both the spiritual and the physical needs of the people around us.

Let me illustrate the importance of integration of the physical and spiritual from a CHE ministry in Papua New Guinea. When CHE teams began working in cooperation with the national government in the Eastern Highlands Province, the district health officer in one district told me that the government had been trying for thirty years to get the people of his district to use latrines.

"What percentage of the population is using them?" I asked. "Three percent," he replied. He paused, and then added, "And they are all dedicated Christians."

He went on to explain that people in his district believe that evil spirits inhabit human waste and hide in dark corners. To build a latrine to contain human waste was to build a spirit house that nobody would go into.

The worldview and belief system in these villages surfaced again and again as the cause of many of their problems. In another instance, traditional belief held that evil spirits entered homes on the wind. As a consequence, people didn't have windows or ventilate their homes, even though they used open fires in their huts to cook and keep warm at night. They were inhabiting smoke-filled spaces, and therefore suffered unnecessarily from respiratory problems as a result.

Latrines: indicators of spiritual growth

One year after my visit to the Eastern Highlands, I returned to help evaluate the progress of the people's development initiatives. When I arrived, the district health officer told me with joy in his eyes that they had 100 percent compliance. All the people in the district were using latrines! Evidence of this was everywhere; not only were there well-built latrines, but they were landscaped with footpaths and ornamental plants.

I knew that I was seeing not just physical change—something spiritual was happening. When people in these communities embraced building and using latrines, they were making a spiritual decision. They had been able to overcome their fear of evil spirits and were now free to change.

In all my Bible college and seminary training as a church planter, nobody ever taught me that a latrine would be an indicator of spiritual growth! I was taught to measure my success by how many people came to church and how much money was in the offering plate each week.

Without an approach to ministry that integrates the physical and the spiritual, attempts at development are futile in situations where behaviors are anchored in spiritual belief. The same is true of discipleship. Without an approach to ministry that integrates the physical and the spiritual, Jesus becomes the Savior who takes us to heaven, but not the Lord of every area of life.

> **When people in these communities started using latrines, they were making a spiritual decision. Without an approach to ministry that integrates the physical and spiritual, attempts at development are futile when behaviors are anchored in spiritual belief.**

In an animistic society, learning and internalizing the truth that Jesus has disarmed the powers of darkness which deceive and threaten communities and understanding that Christ triumphed over these powers through the cross is vital to living free (see Colossians 2:15). Coming to the realization that spirits don't control the assets of any given community, but that each of us has been made in the image of God and has been given dominion over the earth, is liberating. In this way, community members will see that local resources are theirs to steward for the greater good.

I spent much of my ministry career as a church planter who believed that the true indicators of spiritual growth are prayer, Bible study, church attendance, and giving. It never occurred to me—or, as far as I know, to anyone I studied or worked with—that a latrine could be a measure of spiritual maturity. And I never would have learned this lesson if I had not experienced connecting my faith with concepts of compassion and justice and integrating the secular with the sacred.

In order to minister effectively in these contexts, I needed to learn a new way of thinking and doing. In the next section, I will introduce a tool that helped me enormously in that process.

Wholistic Worldview Analysis

Wholistic Worldview Analysis (WWA) is a tool that CHE workers are using in villages to help a community map its strengths, vulnerabilities, and worldview assumptions. The tool was designed in 1997 by Ravi Jayakaran, while he was working with World Vision, to assist community workers in mapping the multidimensional realities of life in the places where they were living and working. In development circles at the time, the worldview of people living in poverty was emerging as a root cause for many of the struggles being faced by their communities. Community development specialists were wrestling with problems such as how to create spiritual baselines, how to analyze community survival strategies, and how to engage the people of a community as owners and managers in their own development process. Jayakaran's observations from his initial study in India, where he researched and developed Wholistic Worldview Analysis, were shared extensively in the World Vision document "Working with the Poor" (MARC publication).

Anchored in the assumption that communities have cohesive survival strategies, Jayakaran's work provides a method for mapping their physical assets, social relationships, and spiritual realities, viewing them as an integrated whole. By mapping their own strategies, a group of people can gain insight into the beliefs and behaviors that inform their way of life, as well as their vulnerabilities and needs.

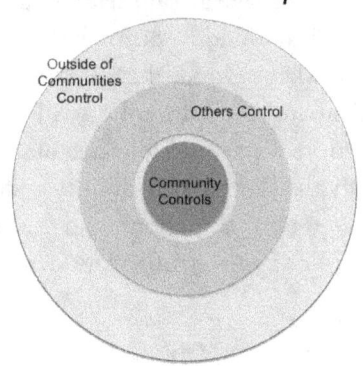

Wholistic Worldview Analysis

This diagram illustrates the structure of survival strategies using concentric circles. In the center circle are resources essential to survival that the people of the community can provide for themselves. Moving from the center out to the next circle, we find resources that the community cannot provide for themselves, but that they get through trade or some other similar means. The outer circle represents things that are essential to the survival of the community, but that the people can neither provide for themselves nor easily acquire. These are a community's vulnerabilities, and—in rural village settings—these are the things that are turned over to the spirits.

My travel and experience in working with villages around the world has led me to conclude that the primary religion of the rural village in the developing world is animism. Many people living in such small communities can name the spirits and gods to which they have turned over their vulnerabilities. There is often somebody in the village—a witchdoctor, sorcerer, soothsayer, or medium—who communicates with the spirits, letting the community know of the spirits' wishes. In addition, since beings from the spiritual realm make themselves known through various methods, villagers set up shrines, perform rituals and ceremonies, and offer sacrifices in an effort to appease these controlling spirits.

As Christians who are engaging these communities with the truth and power of the gospel, we enter into spiritual warfare when we begin to deal with their vulnerabilities. At that point, our work has started to threaten the power of the controlling, demonic spirits and weaken their stranglehold on the community. For that reason, CHE workers often do prayer walks in the communities where they serve.

If we don't deal with the vulnerabilities in these communities, we fail to challenge the people's animistic worldview, and hence we present a truncated gospel. The people may come to understand Jesus to be the Savior who takes away our sins by his death on the cross, but they will fail to see him as the one who disarmed principalities and powers. The result of failing to see the integration of the physical and the spiritual in these contexts is syncretism—a blend of truth and error that adds Jesus to the mix of powers instead of recognizing him as Lord over all of them. Christianity, then, becomes just a veneer over popular animistic beliefs.

> If we don't deal with the vulnerabilities in these communities, we fail to challenge their animistic worldview, and hence present a truncated gospel.

Effective ministry in these contexts requires that we take an approach to address both physical and spiritual concerns simultaneously. Beyond the integration of the physical and the spiritual, it will require that we address the multiple pressures that hold individuals and communities down, including health, education, agriculture, water and sanitation, and business. Addressing these concerns means that we will need to learn to work across the disciplines rather than within them.

Working Across Disciplines Rather Than Within Them

Using the United Nations Development Programme's multidimensional poverty index as a matrix for ministry to the poor, we see immediately that the issue of poverty is complex and that solving it requires a wholistic, multi-sectoral approach.

Consider this scenario: A few years back, an international organization was planning to set up a micro-enterprise program in a target country. Before breaking ground, they conducted a survey of the area. The study revealed that 60 percent of the income of the abject poor in that part of the country was being used to pay for medicines to treat preventable diseases. The organization reasoned that if people received loans for businesses and a relative were to get sick, there was a strong likelihood that the entrepreneurs would spend any earned capital helping their family member to recover. They concluded, then, that in order to do effective micro-enterprise development, health promotion efforts were going to have to be considered as well.

This simple example illustrates the fact that the complex nature of poverty requires a wholistic, integrated response. The complicated issue of poverty, with its many facets, requires us to work across disciplines, such as health promotion and income generation, rather than just unilaterally within them. This means we may need to enter villages as "generalists" rather than as "specialists."

> The complex nature of poverty requires a wholistic and integrated response that works across disciplines rather than within them.

Part of the attractiveness of the CHE strategy is that those entering a community carry with them more than ten thousand lesson plans covering everything from micro-enterprise, disease prevention, and addiction to agriculture, social issues, and Christian discipleship. This assortment of lessons has been developed over three decades as a collection of best practices for community-based development, and they cover just about every problem a worker might encounter in a village. Together, they serve as sort of a reference book. When a problem that needs addressed surfaces in the community, the CHE trainer will pull out the lesson plans on that topic. Then he or she can help the local people identify the causes of that issue and work together to create sustainable, long-term solutions using local resources.

PROCLAIMING CHRIST IN WORD AND DEED

Understanding how the physical and spiritual aspects of life are integrated requires that our message and our work are integrated as well. The gospel of the kingdom that we proclaim embraces every area of life, both physical and spiritual. It must be proclaimed in word *and* deed. The Christ to whom we bear witness is the way, the truth, and the life (John 14:6). He is a compassionate Savior, familiar with our suffering, redeeming all that was lost, and restoring all that was broken by the fall. If we proclaim the truth of Jesus without demonstrating his compassion, have we truly introduced people to Jesus?

> If we proclaim spiritual truth without compassion for physical needs, have we truly introduced people to Jesus?

The evangelism Jesus modeled for us was wholistic. He loved. He was moved with compassion. He cared for both the physical and the spiritual needs of people. Jesus made no separation between word and deed. He taught us to preach the forgiveness of sins *and* to let our light shine before others so that they will see our good deeds and glorify our Father in heaven (Matt 5:16).

Principle 2: Asset-Based Development

Understanding Relief and Development

The first principle of transformational ministry is integration. The second is asset-based development.

In their book *When Helping Hurts*, Steve Corbett and Brian Fikkert define three kinds of intervention, or ways of helping the poor: relief, rehabilitation, and development. They argue that one of the biggest mistakes North American churches make is applying relief in situations in which rehabilitation or development would be the more appropriate intervention.[58]

Crisis situations require disaster relief. The victims of a disastrous event may have an immediate need for water, food, clothing, medical assistance, shelter, and/or other forms of aid—which are usually provided by outsiders who resource and direct the relief effort. Relief activities are short-term, and the primary objective is to save lives. Relief activities are necessary in crisis situations, but they aren't intended to bring long-term solutions to chronic conditions.

Chronic situations, such as poverty, call for a different kind of response. Those living in prolonged poverty need the capacity to create solutions that address the underlying causes of their socioeconomic condition. This kind of activity, referred to as development, is long-term, and the primary objective is to improve quality of life. Good development programs are resourced and controlled by the people themselves, and result in sustainable solutions that aren't reliant on outside resources or support.

One of the keys to helping without hurting is to know when to do what. If we do development when relief is needed, people might die. If we do relief when development is needed, we might create unhealthy dependencies and fail to deliver long-term, sustainable solutions.

Let me share an example of a good development project. CHE trainers had spent months in a community in Central Asia, raising awareness and mobilizing the people to work together against their collective problems. Community leaders were elected to serve on a development committee, and then were trained by the CHE team to identify needs; choose priorities; gather resources; and plan, implement, and evaluate their project.

The highest-priority concern identified by the community leaders was goiter—a swelling of the neck resulting from enlargement of the thyroid gland. In their village of 2,000 residents, 230 goiter cases had been reported in the previous six months. In researching the problem, the community committee discovered

---

58 Steve Corbett and Brian Fikkert, *When Helping Hurts* (Chicago: Moody, 2009).

that the underlying cause for this condition was a lack of iodine in the people's diet. CHE trainers at work in the community responded by educating the locals about goiters and their primary cause.

After a time, the community leaders concluded that the root of the goiter issue was that the salt being sold in their village was not iodized. The obvious solution—to purchase iodized salt—was not without some resistance, however, since iodine-free salt could be obtained at about half the price of the iodized version. Breakthroughs came when community members began to calculate the real cost of the cheaper salt, which included goiter treatment.

> If we do development when relief is needed, people die. If we do relief when development is needed, we create unhealthy dependencies and fail to deliver long-term sustainable solutions.

Understanding the cause of the problem, the development committee, together with the trainers, made a plan. To start, the CHE workers researched a simple and inexpensive way to test for iodine in salt. Armed with the easy-to-use kit, the community leaders tested salt as it was brought to and sold in the community, alerting residents when the salt was bad. Vendors with bad salt began to run away when they saw the leaders coming. Eventually, though, these same vendors returned with good salt. In this way, the goiter problem was solved.

This victory was achieved by the people themselves using local resources. They chose the priorities, created solutions, and carried out their plans. Their solution was sustainable, without dependency on outside resources or support.

While outsiders were involved in the process, they served only as facilitators. The CHE workers raised awareness, inspired hope and vision, mobilized people to work together, and helped the people see what they could do for themselves to solve the problem. They responded to this chronic problem by facilitating a development process. By contrast, if the outsiders had chosen to respond to the issue at hand with a relief-type solution, they would have assessed the community's needs themselves, established their own priorities, blueprinted their own plan, pitched their own solution to donors, and brought in a medical team from the outside to treat the problem. This type of outside intervention would have resolved the problem in the short term, but would have failed to have resolved the problem in the long term.

> If we are going to effectively build capacity for people to own and sustain their own development processes, we ourselves will need to learn a new set of skills.

Developing a New Perspective

The village poor around the world are holding problems in their hands, often not knowing what can be done about these situations. When development workers or good-hearted church members from the West approach these communities wearing shoes that cover the tops of their feet, riding in four-wheel drive vehicles, and having flown into their country on airplanes, the villagers begin to see these outsiders as the solution to their problems. In doing so, they "toss" their problems to the visitor and wait for everything to be resolved.

That "toss" is what I call "the exchange." In that moment, ownership of a problem is transferred from the villager to the visitor. Expectations have been raised in the community, and the outsider now must take care of the issue. The locals put themselves in the place of passive recipients instead of active participants. As a result, the visitor accepts responsibility for solving the problem, using his distant connections and imported resources.

Often what is tossed to the visitor by the village is not a single problem, but a list of problems. When outsiders begin with the question "What do you need?" they invite the villagers to make a wish list, raise expectations among the villagers, and take ownership of the problems themselves.

When an exchange like this takes place, the prospects for sustainable, enduring development die. When villagers hand off their problems to outsiders, the outcome will be services delivered by the outsiders rather than long-term sustainable solutions created by the people themselves. In this way, the outsider has unwittingly, yet with good intention, robbed the local people of their dignity and made them dependents.

Development workers must not allow this "exchange" to take place. It is imperative that they leave any problems being felt by a village in the hands of the people themselves, helping them to understand the causes of their problems and to identify local assets that can be applied to solve them. To avoid the exchange, development workers must avoid the question, "What do you need?" and ask instead, "What do you have?" This will focus villagers on available resources they can use to create solutions and leave ownership of the problem in the locals' hands.

Although "What do you need?" is the wrong question, it is too often where good-hearted people begin. Questions that help the community understand why they have the problems they have and identify resources they can use to solve problems will be much more productive than helping them make a list of needs. In helping others to understand root causes of recurrent problems and encouraging them as they identify assets already in their possession that can be used as part of potential solutions, we are able to inspire a vision for what they can do for themselves. This initiates a process that respects the dignity of the poor and empowers them to create solutions that are both sustainable and multipliable. These kinds of asset-based development solutions are fuel for transformational movements, enabling people not only to do for themselves, but to pass this knowledge along to their neighbors.

> Development workers must avoid the question, "What do you need?" and ask instead, "What do you have?"

If we are going to effectively build capacity for people to own and sustain their own development processes, we ourselves will need to learn a new set of skills. We can no longer drive into a village, do a needs assessment, create solutions, and deliver services. We must learn skills for facilitating processes that empower community members to assess their own needs, understand causes, choose priorities, identify resources, and work together to create appropriate and sustainable solutions. We need to learn and assemble the tools that facilitate human development and not merely the completion of projects.

Changing Our Paradigm

Changing from a needs-based to an asset-based approach will be a true paradigm shift for most of us—a fundamental adjustment in both our methods and our underlying assumptions. It will require that we think and act differently. The chart below contrasts the two approaches.

Needs-Based Approaches	Asset-Based Approaches
Focus on what people lack	Focus on what people have
Results in services delivered by outsiders	Results in sustainable development
Complete projects	Empower people
Create passive recipients or consumers	Create active participants or producers
Reinforce negative mindsets	Restore dignity and build confidence

Needs-based approaches assume that the poor lack resources and need to be provided a solution. Asset-based approaches view the poor as stewards with the capacity to create and deliver solutions themselves. Needs-based approaches make people passive recipients and consumers, while asset-based approaches make them active participants and producers.

Pursuing Different Outcomes That Result in Greater Impact

Moving from a needs-based approach to an asset-based approach also requires that we work toward different outputs and outcomes. Our primary indicators will not be external interventions or deliverables, but internal growth and development in people. This can be illustrated by the following list of desired outcomes in a CHE program. These outcomes are critical to the sustainable development of a community.

- Shared Vision: The community sees a better future and has hope that it can be achieved.
- Leadership: Godly Christian leaders are strategically positioned and equipped to lead the community toward the accomplishment of its vision.
- Ownership: Community members take responsibility for their own health and well-being.
- Cooperation: The community is united and working together for the common good.
- Volunteerism: Significant numbers of community members take initiative and act sacrificially to meet the legitimate needs of others.
- Dignity: The community has recovered its identity as created in the image of God and its vocation as stewards of resources.
- Learning, Skills, and Resources: Community members are equipped to identify needs and local resources, assemble a plan of action, mobilize volunteers to accomplish a vision, and continually reflect on the effectiveness of the process.
- Christian Community and Witness: Believers are meeting for Bible study, prayer, fellowship, and worship, and are sharing Christ with their neighbors in word and deed.

> **People-centered rather than project-centered outcomes increase a community's capacity for growth and development and multiply impact.**

The desired outcomes in the list above are people-centered rather than project-centered. Integrated, or wholistic, people-centered outcomes increase a community's capacity for growth and development and bring about long-term and sustainable impact. Churches are established and strengthened; the overall health of a village improves; infant mortality rates decrease; agriculture becomes more productive; jobs are created; and water systems, roads, schools, and clinics are built. Even more significant are the evidences of peace, justice, compassion, and righteousness in the community, through which God is glorified.

Hal and Lana Jones, colleagues and friends of mine, shared photos that brilliantly contrast the power of an asset-based approach with that of a needs-based approach. In the first photo are people in Gambela, Kenya, standing in front of a simple warehouse which had been built for storing bumper crops of onions. The project was funded by a well-intentioned philanthropist. Lana observed, however, as she presented me with other photographs, that the money coming in from the outside actually limited the vision of the community in Gambela.

Gambela, Kenya Warehouse   Saneba, Burkina Faso Warehouse

By contrast, Lana had seen a people-centered outcome in one of the poorest villages in Saneba, Burkina Faso. This massive warehouse in Saneba (as seen in the photo below) stood in her mind as an amazing contrast to the limited vision of the project-centered approach in Gambela. The building in Saneba was constructed entirely by the community itself and did not use any outside money or difficult-to-obtain resources. Instead, applying what had been learned through an asset-based approach, the local people built an impressive structure that not only provided what was truly needed, but stood as a testament to what they could do if they worked together.

Let me summarize this section on asset-based development with a comment from the vice president of Liberia, Joseph Boakai, who served under President Ellen Johnson Sirleaf from 2006 to 2018. On a trip to Liberia in June of 2012, Larrie Fraley, missions pastor at Christ's Church of the Valley (CCV) in Phoenix, Arizona, arranged for a brief meeting with Vice President Boakai on our way out of the country. We shared CCV's plans for leadership development and CHE with the vice president. He responded by welcoming us, and then he said, "The problem in our country is that our people view development as something *outsiders will do for them* rather than something that *they will do for themselves.*"

> "The problem in our country is that our people view development as something outsiders will do for them rather than something that they will do for themselves."
> —Joseph Boakai,
> Vice President of Liberia

Vice President Boakai put his finger on the problem with needs-based approaches. Thus, in order to correct the assumption that development is something "outsiders will do for them," we need to shift our paradigm from needs-based to asset-based approaches.

Principle 3: Community Ownership

The Biblical Basis for Community Ownership

Community-owned projects are conceived of and controlled by the people themselves. They assess their own needs, choose priorities, set goals, make plans, gather resources, implement solutions, and evaluate outcomes. Conversely, projects that are donor-driven or controlled by outsiders are the opposite of community-owned. When an outsider steps in and does for someone what they should be doing for themselves, they actually impede that person's growth and development and limit the potential for productivity in the long term.

Community ownership from a Christian perspective could be defined as people working together and claiming their God-given responsibility to steward the resources and care for the environment God has entrusted to them. God made male and female in his image and set them apart from the rest of the creation. Then God blessed them and commanded them to be fruitful, multiply, and to *take dominion* over his creation (Genesis 1:28). God created people in his image as stewards of his resources which he entrusted to their care.

God intends for those made in his image to be stewards of resources rather than victims of circumstance. He made people to rule over his creation, not to be controlled by it. Our care for creation and stewardship of the resources God has entrusted to us is our privilege and responsibility as his image-bearers.

> **Well intentioned projects funded by outside resources can actually limit the vision of the community.**

The fall of the first man and woman into sin ruined much of creation—the ground was cursed and stewarding what was given now involved painful toil and sweat. However, God did not take away the resources hidden in the earth or our human responsibility to find and develop them. There are now thorns and thistles, and the task is tougher, but the need and authority to cultivate the land persists. This responsibility to care for the creation that has been entrusted to us is what theologians sometimes refer to as our vocation—the origins of the concept of work. As such, it imbues every profession with meaning and purpose.

Personal growth and development toward God's ideal, his ultimate intentions for us as people, should inspire personal responsibility and empower people to govern their own lives by making use of the assets God has entrusted to their care. Projects of this kind help the poor to make use of local assets and create solutions that are sustainable and reproducible. Even more, unhealthy dependencies naturally disappear, and people recover their God-given vocation as stewards of the earth.

Encouraging Active Participants Rather Than Passive Recipients

The outcomes of community-owned projects are often intangible: dignity, hope, vision, and unity. But these qualities are essential to lasting change, whether in the life of an individual or in a community. The key to sustainable change is engaging individuals and communities as active participants rather than as passive recipients in their development process.

> The outcomes of community-owned projects are often intangible: dignity, hope, vision, and unity. But these qualities are essential to lasting change.

Let me illustrate how this works out in practice with a couple of stories from different places. The first story is about Linda, a dedicated Christian and government health worker, serving as a CHE trainer in Papua New Guinea. Linda was committed to building the capacity of her people to take responsibility for their own needs. She was determined not to allow her people to think of themselves as dependent, weak, and helpless, but as remarkable beings bearing the image of God and fashioned to be stewards of creation.

Unfortunately, domestic violence had grown to become a serious problem in the area, so Linda brought the women together in an association. She taught them their rights and made plans with them to help each other when violence occurred. She inspired the women to set up a mushroom-growing business so that they could provide for themselves and their children.

One day, a woman from the association (we will call her Mona) came to Linda holding a baby she wanted to adopt. Mona feared she would not be able to afford the child's school fees when it came time to send the young girl to school, so she wondered if the group of women could somehow help.

> Community ownership from a Christian perspective could be defined as people working together and claiming their God-given responsibility to steward the resources God has entrusted to them.

Linda put a few peanuts in the woman's hand and said, "That is your child's school fees. Plant these peanuts in the ground, harvest them, plant them again, and continue this process until you have enough peanuts to pay your daughter's school fees."

Linda would be a source of support for Mona for the long term, but she also knew that if she was going to truly help her friend, she needed to insist that Mona take ownership of the problem herself. Mona did take ownership. During my visit with them, she proudly held up a sack of peanuts—the first harvest from those few she planted.

In another community in Central Asia, a Muslim man came to the CHE team's office brimming with joy. He was the chairman of the CHE committee in his community. I was visiting that day and he couldn't wait for the opportunity to tell me what was happening. The gentleman was obviously sincere: He wasn't just telling *a* story; he was telling *his* story! I made a list as he spoke of the changes that were taking place.

- People had learned how to prevent disease and the health of the community was improving.
- People were motivated to solve problems and were working together to find solutions.
- Malaria, previously infecting 95 percent of the community, had nearly been eliminated.
- Young ladies were learning to sew and were finding meaningful employment.
- Young men were learning livelihood skills, such as welding and repairing televisions and sewing machines.
- Thirty families had been properly connected to electricity.

I asked the chairman to tell me the story of how they got electricity to those thirty homes. He explained how the committee assessed the need, determined what materials were required, and then put together a detailed proposal. Then they committed to contribute to the project what they could themselves before seeking funding. In the end, the committee worked with local agencies to put up twenty electric poles and properly connect the two and a half dozen homes. I knew this was only the beginning for this community. The hope, vision, and enthusiasm this small success had generated would propel them to even bigger projects in the future.

In our zeal to fix problems, Westerners often miss out on hearing success stories like these. If the CHE team had brought in a short-term team to provide electricity for the community, I would never have heard this man tell *his* story. Instead of hearing him celebrate his victory and watching him move on to the next project, I might have heard him express gratitude for outside help and then wait passively for the next handout. I heard him tell *his* story because the CHE team refused to take ownership of the community's problems. Instead they helped them to take ownership themselves and to create their own solutions using local resources.

Local Ownership and Contextualization

In my traditional church-planting days, we spent a lot of time thinking and talking about "contextualization." The question was, "How can we, as outsiders to the culture, contextualize our approach so that the churches we plant are adapted to the culture and context of the people?" I see now that our underlying assumptions were wrong. We assumed that we would take ownership of the church plant, and then at some point down the road turn it over to nationals.

> I wish I had understood the principle of community ownership as a church planter. It would have allowed those I served to catalyze church planting movements rather than take over the one "contextualized" church I planted.

I wish I would have understood, as a church planter, the principle of "community ownership." It would have allowed those I served to catalyze national church-planting movements rather than take control of a single "contextualized" church that I had planted. It turns out that the answer to the question we were asking ourselves wasn't really about contextualization at all, but about community ownership.

Principle 4: Multiplication

A Movement That Changed the World

The first principle of transformational movements is integration. The second is asset-based development, and the third is local ownership. The fourth principle, which we will consider now, is multiplication.

The task that Jesus left in the hands of his small band of disciples was not just to reach the person down the street, or to fill up a church building. Jesus commissioned his followers to make disciples of all nations (Matt 28:19–20). The vision Jesus set before his disciples would require them to launch a movement by multiplying disciples beginning in Jerusalem and reaching to the ends of the earth.

His command to make disciples was not intended to be an invitation to a staff position in a church. The command was not just to clergy. Jesus is enlisting all who claim to follow him as volunteers in his service. Each individual commits voluntarily to obey everything that Jesus commanded, and encourages others to do the same.

Jesus' vision is large, but his strategy is simple—obey and multiply. He said that the kingdom of God would be like a little leaven that works itself through the whole lump of dough (Matt 13:33–34). The process of making disciples of all nations could not be accomplished by those first twelve disciples alone. They would need to reproduce and multiply in order to achieve the depth and breadth of the vision he left for them. His vision is deep: transforming lives, communities, and cultures from the inside out. His vision is long: extending from generation to generation. His vision is wide: starting from Jerusalem and working its way to the ends of the earth.

Volunteers and Champions

Jesus initiated a volunteer movement when he commissioned his disciples to make disciples of all nations. His followers would take up their cross, not because they were paid to do it, but because they were compelled by his love. They would champion the cause of Christ and turn the world upside down.

> **Followers of Jesus take up their cross, not because they are paid to, but because they are compelled by his love.**

I met some of his volunteers in the Philippines, turning their world upside down in a densely populated urban slum. One hot, dreary Sunday afternoon, I visited a crowded settlement in metro Manila. A patchwork of makeshift shelters constructed of cardboard, rice sacks, bamboo, and other scavenged materials littered the land. Squatters protected their space in crowded, unsanitary conditions. As I walked into their shanty town, I felt hopelessness and despair in my spirit. I had seldom seen such scarcity and hardship.

About a dozen volunteer CHEs gathered to meet me at a small church on the edge of the shanty town. These women had come to the Lord through our ministry and had been trained to set up micro-businesses. They were studying the Bible together, and were being taught basic principles of health, sanitation, and hygiene. Every woman was assigned a small number of homes to visit regularly in order to share what they were learning with the rest of the community. I listened as each one proudly told of the small business enterprises they had undertaken. They walked me to their homes and showed me what they were doing: one lady made dolls, another sold frozen meats, yet another sold candy. Later, they took me to the homes of people they were ministering to through home visits. I would not have seen the whole significance of their small businesses had I not gone with them on these additional tours.

Next, the CHEs took me to a men's "dormitory" where they ministered to men affected by leprosy and living in unhygienic conditions. While some had minor handicaps, all received food rations from the government. At the time of our visit, a couple of the men stood watching a Christian broadcast on an old television in an otherwise vacant room; the majority were outside gambling. We walked through numerous narrow, smelly alleyways, strewn with tables where men and women gambled what little they had—each one hoping that the next turn of the card would change their fate. It didn't. It never does. It was clear all ambition was gone, and all productive activity had stopped. Life was going nowhere. Nevertheless, these volunteers gave what they had so that they might inspire hope and vision.

Afterward, one of the CHEs insisted that I go to the home of a family to which she ministered. We followed as she took us to a cardboard hut on the edge of a cliff where a woman lived with her eight children. At the bottom of the cliff, perhaps fifty feet below the floor of the hut, was an open sewer made of cement. I noticed a large hole in one of the walls at the back of the hut, overlooking the sewer at the edge of the cliff. The only thing that could be noted inside the woman's space was a small green tub of laundry waiting to be washed by hand—she had absolutely nothing. There was no place for food storage, no stove, and no beds for any of the malnourished children with runny noses and skin infections living there. Absolute destitution!

As we ducked and entered through the door, this mother of eight told me her story. About a year earlier her husband, working on a construction site, was shot and killed by drug addicts. As if that weren't tragic enough, a few weeks later one of her young children fell through the hole in the back wall, splitting his head open on the cement below. He, too, had died. I left that house thinking, "With all the resources available to me, I can't save one family like this from extreme poverty, and there are so many families here. How can I expect these simple volunteers, struggling themselves for survival, to be of any assistance at all to this destitute community?"

Then it hit me like lightning. The CHEs in Manila had already taken their first steps toward freedom. They were not dependent on some outside source, nor were they looking for any monetary rewards for their service to others. They were trusting God and taking responsibility to improve the quality of their lives and empowering others to do the same. They had a shared vision to transform their community, and their little successes were giving hope to all living there. The witness of these CHEs was inspiring others to follow their example, get up, and begin the walk out of extreme poverty.

John Maxwell has said, "I teach what I know, but I reproduce what I am."[59] I might have taught the slum dwellers that day what I know, but that probably wouldn't have brought much hope. After all, I had an education and access to resources they could likely never attain. On the other hand, the dedicated volunteers that were a part of that community were reproducing themselves and inspiring hope in others through their acts of service.

It was their love for Christ and for their neighbor that was motivating these volunteers, not money or any other material-based promise. I saw CHEs who were unstoppable, unrelenting, persistent, and persevering in the work they felt called to do. They were champions whom God was using to bring hope and help to their fellow slum dwellers.

---

59 John Maxwell, *The Power of Thinking Big* (Washington, DC: Eagle Publishing, 2001), 85.

Many believe that the poor who scrape, toil, and struggle just to get by will not willingly become a volunteer. My experience teaches me that the opposite is true. Champions among the poor do take initiative and act voluntarily! They aren't taking action because an outsider is paying them, but because they believe that what they are doing is in their best interest and in the interest of their community. They are compelled not just by the need to survive, but by their compassion for others.

There is a great lesson here for us all. We are called to be champions in the space that God has placed us. We *are called* to serve others, and to bear witness to Christ in word and deed. We should reflect the values of the kingdom of God in our homes, schools, communities, businesses, classrooms, and statehouses. We all, each one of us, has a part to play in Jesus' great movement.

Movements Rather Than Projects

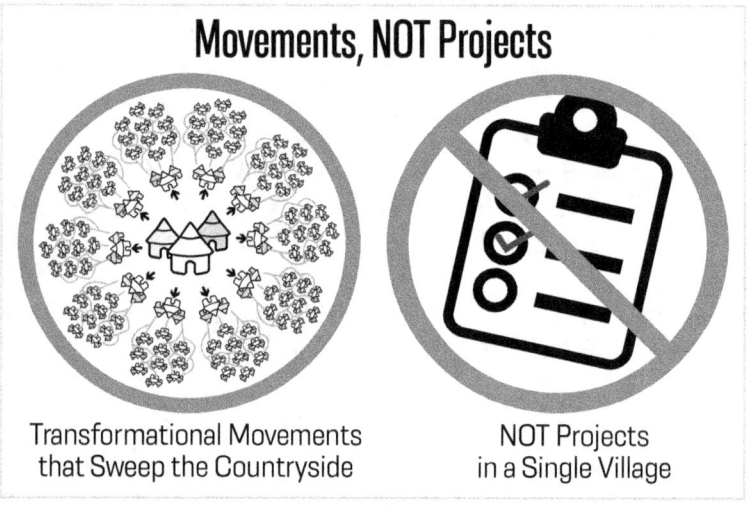

I had a conversation a while back with the chairman of the missions committee in my home church. At one point, he asked me how the church in North America was doing in terms of mission. I hesitated, as I wasn't sure my honesty would be totally appreciated. After saying as much, the chairman encouraged a truthful observation, so I replied that my impression was that the typical church in North America is largely out of touch with the great movements of God in our time. Many churches now define "mission" as short-term projects that they do on behalf of others, and therefore they are missing out on the opportunity to launch movements.

If we view our mission endeavors as projects to finish rather than movements that are beginning, then we have lost sight of something fundamental to our calling. Our mission is not to finish projects, but to make disciples of all nations. Here are a few questions we might want to ask ourselves about potential mission endeavors in order to help us discern whether or not our efforts are consistent with our calling:

1. Will our efforts contribute to a movement of multiplying disciples, or will they just be the sum of several small projects?
2. Can what we are doing be multiplied by those we are serving without input from the outside?
3. Are we creating dependencies on outside resources that will eventually slow the progress of the gospel, or are we encouraging the unleashing of local resources for the cause of Christ?
4. Are we using methods that make people passive recipients, or are they becoming active participants in the cause?

Our commission is one of teaching and training. Jesus has not only commanded us to do things for others, but also to teach others to do for themselves. Our methods should include strategies and processes for passing on vision, skills, and knowledge to all those we interact with, whether it be a neighboring community or the next generation. That is why the Apostle Paul instructed his apprentice, Timothy, to entrust what he learned from Paul to reliable people who would subsequently teach others (2 Tim 2:2).

We will see in the next chapter that Jesus not only entrusted his disciples with the responsibility of discipling others, but he used stories and parables that were easily remembered and transferable. These two strategies employed by Jesus and his disciples—transferable concepts and multiplying trainers—are essential to movements that advance from place to place, culture to culture, and generation to generation. We must employ these strategies ourselves if we are to make movements that change the world.

> If we view our mission endeavors as projects to finish rather than movements that are beginning, then we have lost sight of something fundamental to our calling.

Principle 5: Self-Discovery

Teaching Like Jesus

We have looked at four principles of transformational movements—integration, asset-based development, local ownership, and multiplication. We are now ready to look at the fifth and final principle: self-discovery.

On one occasion, Jesus attracted crowds so large that he had to climb into a boat and push out into the Sea of Galilee to continue teaching them (Mark 4:1). On several occasions, vast numbers of people stayed with Jesus in deserted places until very late and without food in order to engage with him in learning (Matt 14:13-31). Jesus never wrote a book, but his teachings have been memorialized and have changed countless lives throughout the ages.

Regardless of this popularity, Jesus was intent on ministering to those around him through personal relationship. He regularly taught his apostles in more intimate settings, preparing and equipping them for extraordinary ministry that would ultimately change the world. He met individuals, such as the woman at the well and Nicodemus, where they were and transformed their lives through these encounters (John 3, 4).

Jesus led those he taught to participate actively in their own growth, engaging his listeners as students and learners.[60] He commanded his followers to do the same, that they might make disciples of all nations (Matt 28:19–20). In this, Jesus assumed that each person was capable of catalyzing a movement that would dramatically change the world and that their teaching would be transformative. And so, while the disciples learned truth from the master teacher, they also learned the methods he used. I assume that in the same way they carried the content of his message, they also imitated Jesus' delivery.

I want to be careful not to overstate the importance of our teaching methods. There are many things about Jesus that need to be taken into consideration as we calculate the impact of his life, such as the miracles he performed and his resurrection from the dead. Having said that, I have come to believe from experience that there is much we can learn from Jesus about how to teach in ways that engage our listeners as learners who discover truth which then leads to changes in their thinking and behavior.

Much of what I am about to share is drawn from the article "What Can Jesus Teach Us about Student Engagement?" published in the *Journal of Catholic Education* in September 2015. The authors—Glenn James, Elda Martinez, and Sherry Herbers—describe the following four elements evident in Jesus' teaching process, patterns in Jesus' teaching methodology that led to transformational learning in the context of an enduring relationship between teacher and peer:

1. A disorienting dilemma
2. Questioning of assumptions
3. Reflection
4. A call to action

Let's explore these four elements of Jesus' teaching methodology and see how these strategies engaged his hearers as students in a learning process that changed their perspectives and behaviors.

---

[60] Glenn James, Elda Martinez, and Sherry Herbers, "What Can Jesus Teach Us about Student Engagement?" *Journal of Catholic Education* (September 2015).

Disorienting Dilemmas

James, Martinez, and Herbers tell us that transformation usually begins when an individual's assumptions or beliefs have been challenged. Challenged assumptions often create an uncomfortable dissonance, or even a state of disequilibrium in which a person feels that the assumptions and beliefs currently operative in their lives are inadequate for dealing with the dilemmas they face. Teachers that facilitate thinking and change often pose dilemmas that may create strong feelings of doubt, confusion, and even anger. These disorienting dilemmas challenge the learner's assumptions and force them to grapple with the question of whether their beliefs and operative assumptions are adequate to answer the questions posed by the dilemma. Here are some disorienting dilemmas from the teaching of Jesus that challenged cultural assumptions or beliefs and created discomfort in the minds of his hearers:

- "Follow me, and let the dead bury their own dead" (Matt 8:22).
- "Whoever finds their life will lose it, and whoever loses their life for my sake will find it" (Matt 10:39 2011 NIV).
- "Don't you see that whatever enters the mouth goes into the stomach and then out of the body? But the things that come out of a person's mouth come from the heart, and these defile them" (Matt 15:17–18 2011 NIV).
- "If your eye causes you to sin, gouge it out and throw it away. It is better for you to enter life with one eye than to have two eyes and be thrown into the fire of hell" (Matt 18:9 2011 NIV).
- "Foxes have dens and birds have nests, but the Son of Man has no place to lay his head" (Matt 8:20 2011 NIV).
- "Come to me, all you who are weary and burdened, and I will give you rest. Take my yoke upon you and learn from me, for I am gentle and humble in heart, and you will find rest for your souls. For my yoke is easy and my burden is light" (Matt 11:28–30 2011 NIV).
- "Make a tree good and its fruit will be good, or make a tree bad and its fruit will be bad, for a tree is recognized by its fruit" (Matt 12:33).
- "Again I tell you, it is easier for a camel to go through the eye of a needle than for someone who is rich to enter the kingdom of God" (Matt 19:24).
- "But I want you to know that the Son of Man has authority on earth to forgive sins." So he said to the paralyzed man, "Get up, take your mat and go home" (Matt 9:6).
- "Let any one of you who is without sin be the first to throw a stone at her" (John 8:7).

Each of these statements would have created a disorienting dilemma for Jesus' audience. The last two verses alone are sufficient to illustrate that point. When Jesus claimed to have the authority to forgive sins and then healed a paralyzed man to reinforce his point, he created a dilemma in the minds of the teachers of the law who had assumed that Jesus was not divine. By saying, "Let any one of you who is without sin be the first to throw a stone at her," Jesus made the self-righteous teachers of the law and Pharisees who were ready to judge a woman caught in adultery uncomfortable with condemning her to death.

Jesus used situations and stories to pose problems. With each story or situation, he visualized a real problem faced by the community and called the participants to think through the issue, discover truth, and resolve the dilemma for themselves.

Questioning Assumptions

After presenting a disorienting dilemma, Jesus often used questions to challenge assumptions and engage participants in seeking out a solution. In the Gospels, Jesus asked many more questions than he answered. Martin Copenhaver points this out in his book title: *Jesus Is the Question: The 307 Questions Jesus Asked and the 3 He Answered*. Copenhaver observes that Jesus asked 307 questions; and conversely, Jesus was asked 183 questions by others. And of those 183 questions Jesus was asked, he directly answered only three. Asking questions was central to Jesus' teaching process. He used questions to throw the burden of discovery back on the hearers, requiring them to engage as students and learners and to find a resolution to the challenge his questions posed. As Copenhaver puts it: "Through Jesus' questions, he modeled the struggle, the wondering, the thinking it through that helps us draw closer to God and better understand, not just the answer, but ourselves."[61] Here are some of the questions Jesus asked that challenged the assumptions of the people he addressed:

"If you love those who love you, what reward will you get? Are not even the tax collectors doing that? And if you greet only your own people, what are you doing more than others? Do not even pagans do that?" (Matt 5:46–47 2011 NIV).

- "Is not life more than food, and the body more than clothes?" (Matt 6:25 2011 NIV).
- "Can any one of you by worrying add a single hour to your life?" (Matt 6:27 2011 NIV).

---

61 Martin B. Copenhaver, *Jesus Is the Question: The 307 Questions Jesus Asked and the 3 He Answered* (Nashville: Abingdon, 2014).

- "How can you say to your brother, 'Let me take the speck out of your eye,' when all the time there is a plank in your own eye?" (Matt 7:4 2011 NIV).
- "You of little faith, why are you so afraid?" Then he got up and rebuked the winds and the waves, and it was completely calm (Matt 8:26 2011 NIV).
- "How can the guests of the bridegroom mourn while he is with them? The time will come when the bridegroom will be taken from them; then they will fast" (Matt 9:15 2011 NIV).
- "If any of you has a sheep and it falls into a pit on the Sabbath, will you not take hold of it and lift it out?" (Matt 12:11 2011 NIV).
- "Who is my mother, and who are my brothers?" (Matt 12:48 2011 NIV).
- "What good will it be for someone to gain the whole world, yet forfeit their soul? Or what can anyone give in exchange for their soul?" (Matt 16:26 2011 NIV).
- "Shouldn't you have had mercy on your fellow servant just as I had on you?" (Matt 18:33 2011 NIV).

Each of these questions challenged operative assumptions in the minds of the hearers. Reflection on these questions would not only lead to a new way of thinking, but to a new way of living.

Reflection

In a unique way, Jesus used parables to call his hearers to reflect, make a decision, and act. He often left the conclusion to his parables open-ended, allowing his listeners to see themselves in the story and write the ending into their own lives by consciously deciding to change their thinking and behavior.

> Jesus often left the conclusion to his parables open-ended, allowing his listeners to see themselves in the story and write the ending into their own lives.

Copenhaver notes that well-known scholar C. S. Dodd, in his book *The Parables of the Kingdom*, observes that Jesus used parables to leave sufficient doubt so as to tease the mind into active thought.[62] Likewise, Felix Just, in his study of Jesus' parables, reaches a similar conclusion. He points out that most parables are open-ended, challenging us to keep thinking.[63] By choosing this method, Jesus invites his hearers to reflect and to write the ending of the story in their own lives.

The parables Jesus told often dealt with controversial themes and "shatter the structures of our accepted world."[64] As was noted earlier, they present disorienting

---

62 Ibid.
63 Ibid.
64 Copenhaver quotes Reid, *A Wonderful Book* (New York: Great Books Publishing, 2001), 8.

dilemmas. However, because a parable appears to be about other people, the hearers are more likely to be open and willing to explore the controversial themes the story introduces. The distance allows the listener to see more clearly what is right, and then shines a light on their own assumptions, thereby creating a need for decision and change. Parables remove our defenses, allow us the space to think about the structures of our accepted world, and invite us to change our ways.

In Matthew 13:13–14, Jesus describes those who see the need for change with clarity through his parables, yet refuse to take action, as people who hear but do not understand:

"This is why I speak to them in parables:
'Though seeing, they do not see;
though hearing, they do not hear or understand.'

"In them is fulfilled the prophecy of Isaiah:

'You will be ever hearing but never understanding;
you will be ever seeing but never perceiving.'"

When Jesus told a parable, the reality was not that those listening were incapable of understanding the parable. Instead, their prejudice and worldview assumptions wouldn't allow them to make the intended application. Jesus challenged people to stop and think, knowing that such reflection would only stir up hostility in hearers who strongly opposed the truth he taught.

One of Jesus' best-known parables is the parable of the prodigal son. While we tend to focus on the prodigal, the story was actually told with emphasis on the son who had stayed home. We find the context for the telling of this parable in Luke 15:1–2 (2011 NIV): "Now the tax collectors and sinners were all gathering around to hear Jesus. But the Pharisees and the teachers of the law muttered, 'This man welcomes sinners and eats with them.'"

The disorienting dilemma presented in this parable is the unwillingness of the son who stayed home to welcome his brother home in the same way as his father. The parable ends with the father saying to the older son, "My son, you are always with me, and everything I have is yours. But we had to celebrate and be glad, because this brother of yours was dead and is alive again; he was lost and is found" (Luke 15:31–32).

The Pharisees' assumptions were being challenged, and through this parable Jesus made it clear to them that their refusal to welcome tax collectors and sinners was inconsistent with the Father's will. Jesus didn't conclude the parable by telling us how the older son responded to his father's admonishment. He wanted the Pharisees to write the conclusion in their own lives. As they considered the untold ending, they might have envisioned several ways in which the older son could have possibly responded. Perhaps he went to the party and welcomed the brother home. Maybe he boycotted the party and refused to celebrate the return of his lost brother. Or it might be that he tried to stop the party altogether, calling on others not to associate with the sinner.

The application here isn't just for the Pharisees who refused to welcome tax collectors and sinners. Jesus invites *us* to write the ending in *our own* lives. How will we treat "sinners"? Will we go to the party, boycott it, or try to stop it?

A Call to Action

Jesus was learner centered. Rather than abstract ideas, his teachings were aimed at specific problems to which his hearers needed to respond. He calls people to action.

We live in a culture, though, that is perhaps as far removed from that of ancient Israel as any in history. Yet Jesus' calls for action are as relevant to us today as they were during his time on earth two millennia ago. His truth rings out

> Jesus challenged people to stop and think, knowing that such reflection would only stir up hostility in hearers who strongly opposed the truth he taught.

from the past and echoes in the present with remarkable clarity and relevance. The disorienting dilemmas he used then are still disorienting today because they often contradict our worldview assumptions. The questions he asked then still challenge our assumptions and beliefs today, and reflection on those questions will lead us not only to change our thinking, but our behavior and way of life as well.

Jesus challenges our individualism and striving for self-actualization with a call to deny ourselves, take up our cross, and follow him. He says, "Whoever finds their life will lose it, and whoever loses their life for my sake will find it" (Matt 10:39 2011 NIV).

Jesus challenges our materialism by asking, "What good will it be for someone to gain the whole world, yet forfeit their soul? Or what can anyone give in exchange for their soul?" (Matt 16:26). And "Is not life more than food, and the body more than clothes?" (Matt 6:25 2011 NIV).

Jesus challenges our so-called boundaries with his love and forgiveness. When Peter asked, "Lord, how many times shall I forgive my brother or sister who sins against me? Up to seven times?" Jesus answered, "Not seven times, but seventy-seven times" (Matt 18:21–22 2011 NIV).

Jesus challenges our hatred for oppressors with calls to love our enemies, do good to those who hate us, and pray for those who persecute us (Matt 5:43–48).

Jesus challenges our relativism with truth. Jesus declared, "You will know the truth, and the truth will set you free" (John 8:32).

And Jesus doesn't stop there; he continues to get to the heart of the matter. He challenges our agnosticism with his miracles. He claimed to be the resurrection and the life, and then raised Lazarus from the dead (John 11:25–44). He claimed to be the light of the world, and then healed a man born blind (John 8:12; 9:1–11).

He fed five thousand men, and then claimed to be the bread of life (John 6:1–13, 35). He walked on water and calmed the storm, convincing his disciples that he truly was the Son of God (Matt 14:32–33).

Engaging Listeners as Learners

As I reviewed Jesus' teaching processes and how his processes engaged hearers as students and led to changes in belief and behavior, I couldn't help but compare that to what I was taught about homiletics in Bible college and seminary. I wondered why these concepts were never even explored. My experience with these principles has itself been a disorienting dilemma that has caused me to ask some hard questions in regard to assumptions I have had about preaching and teaching.

> Jesus' teachings were aimed at specific problems to which the hearers needed to respond. In so doing, he called people to action.

Do our sermons compel people to "stop thinking" or to "stop and think"? Do our preferred teaching styles raise questions in the minds of the hearers and leave them with enough doubt to search the Scriptures, think through issues, and discover answers for themselves? Do we have the courage to question cultural assumptions, knowing that this will likely make people uncomfortable and perhaps hostile? Are we willing to shatter the structures of our hearers' world so that they might have ears to hear the truth of God? Are we interesting storytellers who invite our hearers to see themselves in the story, compelling them to write the end of the story in their own lives? Are we calling people to action, or simply to come to our church building again next week? Do we meet people on the streets and engage them with real-life dilemmas?

> Do our lectures and sermons call people to "stop thinking" or to "stop and think?"

The last command that Jesus gave before ascending to his Father was to "go and make disciples of all nations, baptizing them in the name of the Father and of the Son and of the Holy Spirit, and teaching them to obey everything I have commanded you" (Matt 28:19–20). Jesus not only expects us to take action, but to encourage others to do the same. That command should challenge us to think seriously about the outcomes Jesus was looking for in his followers and about the processes he used to get there.

My hope and prayer is that I have raised enough questions to challenge you to explore the teaching methods of Jesus yourself and to engage your hearers as students. May you be determined to teach like Jesus—presenting disorienting dilemmas that challenge the cultural assumptions of your hearers and lead them to reflect, discover new insights, and take action leading to growth and development in their own lives and in the communities in which they live.

Teaching the CHE Way

I have been using the CHE (Community Health Evangelism) teaching methodology of participatory learning for more than twenty years. I have used it simply because it works. Time and again, I witness people leave our training with new insights and a passion that changes the whole course of their lives and ministry. I have observed this phenomenon consistently for more than two decades, seeing thousands of people from different backgrounds and cultures inspired and mobilized by what they discovered in our seminars.

In 2018 I was invited to speak on the topic of participatory learning at the International Wholistic Missions Conference at Grand Canyon University in Phoenix, Arizona. I accepted the invitation thinking that I would just speak from my experience. But in preparation for that talk, I came across the article written by James, Martinez, and Herbers, which was the basis of what I just presented. In reading the results of their research, I had an "Aha moment!"—an inspiring revelation, so to speak. CHE didn't invent this method of teaching; Jesus used it two thousand years ago!

The CHE approach, being used by practitioners all around the world, bears a striking resemblance to the teaching process of Jesus. CHE facilitators are trained to pose issues, challenge assumptions, invite reflection and self-discovery, and call hearers to action. CHE is especially suited to villages, but people who have taken our training often tell me that they are using it in classrooms, Bible studies, and pulpits.

CHE training is intended to empower individuals and communities to be architects of their own development. The CHE trainer doesn't deliver prepackaged solutions in the style of a lecture, but rather facilitates discussions that involve the people brainstorming together and creating their own solutions. The chart below compares these two approaches to learning and teaching.

Lecture (Traditional Approach)	Discussion (The CHE Way)
Content-Focused	Learner-Centered
Gives advice	Raises awareness
Participants listen	Participants respond
Outsiders own solutions	Insiders own solutions
Projects, if undertaken, are accomplished by outsiders	Projects are accomplished by insiders

Instead of blueprinting solutions and lecturing to the community about what to do, CHE facilitators pose problems (disorienting dilemmas) that often challenge cultural assumptions. For example, they might act out a skit about an individual drinking dirty water and then having stomach problems.

The people will identify with the ailments, but the connection to dirty water creates a disorienting dilemma for those among them who believe that disease is caused by spirits.

Once the problem is posed, we work through a series of questions, beginning with "Why is this happening?" and concluding with "What are we going to do about it?" The participants will break into small groups for parts of the discussion to reflect on their experiences with the problem, explore case studies, study evidence, and then report their discoveries to the larger group. As the process unfolds, the group builds consensus together and creates an action plan. This methodology is easy to learn and can be adapted for use in many different contexts.

> The CHE approach to learning, being used by practitioners all around the world, bears a striking resemblance to the teaching process of Jesus.

In the next chapter I will share inspiring stories of transformation that I gathered from my travels as a consultant to CHE teams around the world. These stories highlight extraordinary people, events, and outcomes as the movement spread rapidly from community to community and from country to country. Underlying all these activities and achievements is the "CHE way" of teaching, similar to what Jesus used, that engages community members in processes of self-discovery that lead to action. This methodology can be used in any ministry and will be useful in any learning environment—whether a school, church, Bible study, or community project.

CHAPTER 7
Change That Informs and Inspires—Stories of Transformation

At Medical Ambassadors International, I was privileged to come alongside a group of committed change-makers who were catalyzing CHE movements all around the globe. Visiting CHE ministries in more than sixty countries gave me an inside look at the village transformation taking place as a result.

> In just four years, nearly ten thousand people came to Christ in CHE programs in the Philippines, and whole communities were lifted out of cycles of poverty and disease. The movement spread from there to nine other countries in Southeast Asia and the Pacific.

In 1997 I was hired by Medical Ambassadors International to coordinate CHE work in the Philippines, with a view to expanding MAI's efforts into Southeast Asia. I worked alongside Filipinos for five years, opening ministries in nine new countries. In 2002 I became the regional coordinator for South Asia, Southeast Asia, and the Pacific; and in 2004 I was appointed the international coordinator.

Through my engagement with Medical Ambassadors, I was privileged to come alongside an international group of committed change-makers who were catalyzing CHE movements all around the globe. Visiting CHE ministries in more than sixty countries gave me an inside look at the change that was taking place, as a result of CHE work.

In this chapter I am going to share about one stream of the CHE movement that began in remote villages in the Philippines and spread from there throughout Southeast Asia and to many other countries around the world. All of my colleagues at Medical Ambassadors have their own stories to tell—a collection that could fill the pages of a second book.[65]

I will begin by telling the story of change in the first Philippine villages where the CHE strategy was used. These stories will illustrate the depth and breadth of the change that take place in a CHE community. I will then recount what happened in other countries as the movement spread throughout Southeast Asia. The movement has spread so far and wide that it is impossible to tell it all. But the stories from other countries in Southeast Asia will be enough to give us a picture.

---

65 My colleagues at Medical Ambassadors, each with their own story to tell: Stan Rowland, Dr. Gil Odendaal, Charlotte Deuel, Gordon Claassen, Dr. David Sir, Dr. David Jung, John and Charleen McWilliam, Dayo Obaweya, Dr. Hugo Gomez, Tirus and Winnie Githaka, Dr. Bibiana McLeod, Rev. Vic Mendoza, and Dr. Rhodora Mendoza.

The Birth of a Movement: From Rural Philippines to the World

The Republic of the Philippines is an archipelago of 7,641 islands in Southeast Asia. Ninety-five percent of the land area is on just eleven of the islands, which are organized into three geographical divisions from north to south: Luzon, Visayas, and Mindanao. Filipinos are known to be among the friendliest and most welcoming people in all of Asia. Most Filipinos are multilingual. The national language is Tagalog (Filipino) and the trade language is English, but there are twelve major indigenous regional languages with more than a million speakers each. With a population of 110 million people—55.6 percent of them in rural areas and 44.4 percent in cities—the Philippines is the thirteenth most populous country in the world.[66] Of the two hundred different people groups in the Philippines, thirty of them are classified as unreached with the gospel. The majority of the unreached are Muslim people groups on the big island of Mindanao in the south.[67]

When CHE work began in the Philippines in 1991, 53.5 percent of all Filipinos lived on less than two dollars per day.[68] Almost 25 percent did not have access to safe drinking water, and more than 30 percent did not have adequate sanitary facilities. Trapped in a cycle of poverty and disease, the poor in the Philippines had the same concerns as most in the developing world. They needed long-term solutions to their problems—not just food for a day or medicine for the moment. They needed to be instructed in healthy living and taught the importance of clean water, sanitation, hygiene, and adequate nutrition. They needed to know how to make use of available resources to improve the quality of their own lives. They also needed people to live among them, proclaiming the forgiveness of sins and modeling and instructing them in the ways of the Lord.

The stories in this chapter are about the work of Filipino pioneers who championed a commitment to disciple whole communities, one family at a time. They used the CHE model, training and equipping village committees to manage the development process and mobilizing volunteers in every community to make regular home visits. They brought the message of salvation through faith in Christ to individuals, and the values of the kingdom to households and communities. Through their work they multiplied disciples, helped villagers to take responsibility for their own health and well-being, and multiplied that success by training individuals who would also train others. The results were healthier families, more

---

66 "Philippines Population (Live)," Worldometer, http://www.worldometers.info/world-population/philippines-population/.

67 "People Groups: Philippines," Joshua Project, https://joshuaproject.net/countries/RP.

68 Karin Schelzig, "Poverty in the Philippines: Income, Assets, and Access," Asian Development Bank, January 2005, https://www.adb.org/sites/default/files/publication/29763/poverty-philippines.pdf.

self-reliant communities, and new or strengthened churches. As changes became evident in individuals and communities, the work spread from family to family, from community to community, and from country to country.

Between 1997 and 2001, nearly ten thousand people came to Christ, and whole communities were lifted out of cycles of poverty and transformed both physically and spiritually. The CHE workers would go on to champion their cause by teaching others in Southeast Asia what they had learned, catalyzing transformational movements that would spread from there to all around the globe. The movement spread in three ways: (1) From home to home and community to community in the Philippines; (2) From the Philippines to nine more countries in Southeast Asia and the Pacific as these Filipino workers shared their stories and traveled with me to train and equip workers; and (3) By inviting workers from around the world to intern in the Philippines—spending time in these communities and learning to start transformational movements of their own.

> If what happened in the Philippines between 1997 and 2001 were the end of the story, it would be too late to tell it. However, after almost two decades of continuing expansion all around the world, the story is ongoing.

Space will not allow me to tell the whole story, even of the work done in the Philippines. During the period I am recounting, eight teams were at work in the Philippines, making a contribution to establishing models and creating the movement I will describe. I will briefly tell the story of just three of the eight CHE teams at work between 1997 and 2001 when I served as their director: two on the island of Mindanao in the south and one on the island of Panay in the central part of the country.[69] If what happened there were the end of the story, it would be too late to tell it. However, after almost two decades of continuing expansion all around the world, the story is ongoing. Going back to the beginnings will provide both a picture of how this stream of the CHE movement began and insights about how we might catalyze new movements in our spheres of influence today.

Barangay San Antonio, Ozamiz City

First, let's go to a fishing village in Barangay San Antonio, on the shores of Iligan Bay in Ozamiz City in Western Mindanao. The team leaders in Ozamiz City were Dr. Leo Tago (dentistry) and Dr. Mary Tago (family practice). They were accompanied by two nurses, Ann Yap and Analyn Begafria. Committed to one mission, they all shared the same house just a few minutes from the project.

This CHE team witnessed marked improvement in the quality of life for 2,500 squatters in seven different villages (*puroks*) during the time they were serving there. When they first entered the district (*barangay*), people were living

---
69 The other five teams served in metro Manila, Cebu, Davao, Bohol, and Zamboanga.

> The CHE team in Barangay San Antonio witnessed marked improvement in the quality of life for 2,500 people in seven different villages.

idly—drinking, quarreling, gambling at mahjong tables, and participating in cock fights. Little by little, these things began to disappear. The people of Barangay San Antonio began to work together to care for each other's needs.

The CHE committee set twenty-three specific goals for their program in their communities along the seashore. These goals included ensuring that 100 percent of families would have gardens and latrines, that everyone would use garbage cans, that all gambling would cease, and that each person in the community would become God-fearing.

The CHE committee used contests to mobilize their people toward the achievement of many of the proposed goals. They held a "well-baby contest," a "cooking contest" (in search of the most nutritious and inexpensive meals), a "deworming contest," and several others. In the case of this last one, they offered a prize to the person who recorded the greatest number of eliminated worms. One woman gave up more than one hundred worms—meticulously counted!

When I arrived for the first time to evaluate the work, the center of the barangay was decorated with flags along the pathways and handmade posters were on every home. They were holding a day of celebration, complete with a parade, sports fest, and awards ceremonies. The mayor of Ozamiz was the commencement speaker, and the vice mayor gave the closing address. Each of the seven puroks (villages) in the barangay had large processions, with everyone wearing uniforms of some kind or another.

> "Before the CHE program, there was so much shouting in our homes that it was as if every home had megaphones. Now our homes are peaceful."

At a public meeting, I asked the residents of the community to share with me what improvements they had seen in their barangay as a result of the CHE program. Their responses surprised me. I expected them to say that worms, scabies, and impetigo had been nearly eradicated (because they were) or that malnutrition had decreased (because it had). I expected they might say something about the fact that 37 percent of the homes now had latrines and 76 percent had gardens. Instead, the people spoke freely about how they were able to cooperate, how they had grown in their relationship with God, and how gambling in the community had been minimized. Asked specifically about physical improvements in the barangay, one man testified, "Before the CHE program, there was so much shouting in our homes that it was as if every home had megaphones. Now our homes are peaceful."

As I was leaving, a young CHE volunteer named Merlyn approached me. She explained that during the meeting where the community leaders testified to what God was doing in their midst, she wanted to say something but was too shy. Perhaps she didn't feel she had the status to speak up or she was uncomfortable speaking in front of so many people. At any rate, Merlyn was eager to share her perspective on the changes in the community. "The government has tried all kinds of programs in our barangay," she said. "But nothing worked until Dr. Leo and Dr. Mary came. I thank the Lord for them."

God was transforming this entire barangay with seven puroks from the inside out. They had a shared vision for a better future. Leaders were positioned and equipped to lead the community toward the accomplishment of its vision; people were taking responsibility for their own health and well-being and were united and working together for the common good; volunteers were taking initiative and acting sacrificially to meet the legitimate needs of others; and believers were meeting together for fellowship, prayer, Bible study, and worship.

After completing this work in Ozamiz City, Leo and Mary moved to Cambodia to continue their life calling as missionaries, initiating CHE work in villages there.

Barangay Sukailang, Surigao City

> One visiting development worker from India exclaimed, "Now for the first time, I have seen truly sustainable development!

The second team I want to tell you about went to work outside the city of Surigao on the northernmost tip of the island of Mindanao. Led by Dr. Amelia Nambatac (known simply as Mely), the team started doing CHE work in 1989. They pioneered in six different communities in the decade that followed.

During the first six years, between 1989 and 1995, Mely and her team concentrated their efforts on Barangay Sukailang on the outskirts of Surigao City. Many came to Christ, and a beautiful church was built by the people themselves in the heart of the community, on property donated by the Barangay Council. A member of Mely's team was called to serve as their pastor. The Barangay of Sukailang became a model in the province—people came from all around to see the development that had taken place in the different puroks. One visiting development worker from India exclaimed, "Now, for the first time, I have seen truly sustainable development!"

As a result of this team's commitment to community ownership and an asset-based approach, the community, led by the CHE committee, built a water system, a daycare center, a cooperative store, a road, and a bridge connecting their barangay to the main highway. Every home had a latrine and a FAITH (Food Always In The

Home) garden. The progress in this community was so impressive that professionals from the city started buying lots and building homes there. What was once a rural slum was slowly transformed into a middle-class neighborhood.

> A rural slum was slowly transformed into a middle-class neighborhood.

In appreciation for all that Mely's team did in Sukailang, the barangay captain, the highest elected official in the barangay, awarded each member of the team a plot of land on which to build a house (which, of course, they did). This team witnessed what can happen in a community when the truth of God's Word rules in the hearts of people living together in community.

After twelve years, a thorough and objective external evaluation documented the impact of the work of this team. The evaluation revealed that 67 percent of those randomly surveyed in this team's cluster of communities claimed to have prayed to accept Christ as Savior during home visits made by CHE volunteers. Participating households were healthier across a whole set of indicators and were more spiritually focused (more group praying and Bible sharing, increased attendance in worship and other church activities, fewer conflicts, positive attitudes). Villages were "clean and green," demonstrating community-wide collaboration and showing increased self-confidence.[70]

Igdalaquit, Antique

While the two teams I just shared about were pioneering on the southern island of Mindanao, another CHE team was at work catalyzing a transformational movement on the island of Panay in the west-central part of the Philippines. This team of four, Pastor Fred and Mila Gabriel, Beth Torrefiel, and Pastor Ed Blanco, impressed me as very godly men and women with a real heart for their people. (This is the same team that did the work with Mayor Palabrica to transform the town of Bingawan as described in chapter 3). They were working in Igdalaquit, a remote barrio in one of the poorest provinces in the country. Government agencies had rejected Igdalaquit as unfit for development. The people were uncooperative. Families lived in bamboo huts with no sanitation. Men would spend their days drinking and gambling in the streets.

> The CHE teams that pioneered the first programs in Asia began to receive and train leaders from dozens of countries. They used their programs as models and inspired and equipped hundreds of leaders to return to their countries and initiate CHE work all around the world.

---

70 M. B. Amayun and A. Talens, *Community Health Evangelism: Health and Holism for the Philippines' Rural Poor: An Evaluation Report on Medical Ambassadors' Program in Antique and Surigao, the Philippines* (Spring Lake, MI: Rushing Wind Foundation, 2001).

When I visited the barrio seven years after the CHE team began their work, I found a peaceful and quiet barrio. Villagers are now involved in constructive activities rather than vice and are working together for the common good. They live in permanent hollow-block homes with running water, toilets, and proper drainage systems. They have built a health center, established a small pharmacy, and paved their streets. They have beautified their community with fences, plants, trees, and flowers. They are employed in a variety of new livelihood projects, including raising hogs, goats and poultry; making handicrafts; and buying and selling various products.

Word of these changes reached all the way to Malacanang Palace, the official residence and workplace of the president of the Philippines. The community leaders were invited to send a representative to the palace to receive a bronze medal in a province-wide community health and development competition.

A building in the center of Igdalaquit was symbolic of the deep changes taking place there. As people in the village came to Christ and reflected on the future of their community, they felt they were missing three things: a church, a school, and a community center. After considering various solutions, they decided to build just one structure in a centrally located place. They called it the Life Community Learning Center. During the week it was their "kinder-school," in the evenings it was a community center, and on Sundays it was their church. Although not everyone attends the church that meets in the building, the church belongs to the community and is valued by everyone.

The same professional evaluators who documented the work of Mely's team in Surigao visited Antique and observed similarly startling impacts there: 88 percent of those surveyed at random had prayed to receive Christ during home visits made by CHEs, and participating households in the community were healthier and more spiritually active. As in Surigao, participating households were healthier across a whole set of indicators, including being more spiritually focused. They taught about Christ through Bible sharing and prayer meetings, had more caring attitudes and more harmonious relationships, and increased church attendance; overall, they were more God-fearing people. Villages were "clean and green," demonstrating community-wide collaboration and showing increased self-confidence.[71] This external evaluation affirmed that the work these dedicated believers were doing in a remote corner of the world was truly extraordinary, and that their story needed to be told more broadly.

The changes in Igdalaquit were multiplied in other rural poor communities, including Mapatag, another small barangay. I listened as one CHE worker after another testified how they came to faith in Christ through the Community Health Evangelism program and what God was doing through them as a result.

---

71 Ibid.

One young woman, Jovy, told her story: "I was a nagger and used to fight with my husband until he cried! Then I realized what kind of person I was and trusted Christ as my Savior. My husband is also now a believer."

In her written testimony she continues,

> I thought before that my knowledge of God was sufficient. It was not until I became a CHE member that I discovered there were still lots of things I have to learn about God, the Lord Jesus, and his Word. I thank God for the lessons on the assurance of salvation I learned through the CHE program. I praise God for the presence of the Holy Spirit in my life and for his control over my life. Every time I speak filthy words, I can feel the Holy Spirit convicting me of my sins. He also gave me the strength to submit to God's will and obey him. It was not until I knew Christ as my Savior that I realized the real meaning of life.

> "I was a nagger and used to fight with my husband until he cried! Then I realized what kind of person I was and trusted Christ as my Savior. My husband is also now a believer."

Jovy: A CHE Volunteer

From the Philippines to the World

The first CHE internship was established in the Philippines in 2002. The CHE teams that pioneered the first programs in Asia began to receive and train leaders from dozens of countries. They used their programs as models and inspired and equipped hundreds of leaders to return to their countries and initiate CHE work all around the world. Some of their interns not only launched CHE movements in their home countries, but established internships of their own as well.

As I noted earlier, I took Filipinos with me into Southeast Asia to help train and equip teams there for CHE ministry. The Filipino teams with which we partnered named their organization Holistic Community Development and Initiatives (HCDI). Their president, Pastor Vic Mendoza, traveled with me much of the time to other countries in Southeast Asia; and together we mobilized, trained, and equipped others for ministry. Our first stop was Cambodia.

Cambodia: From Killing Fields to Life-Giving Movements

When I arrived in Cambodia for the first time in 1998, the country was still recovering from the Khmer Rouge mass killings that took place between 1975 and 1979 and claimed the lives of one out of every six people. Educated citizens had been considered enemies of the state and cruelly executed. Almost every family had been split up, with children being brainwashed and trained to kill. Cambodians today understandably find this period so painful that most cannot speak about it.

"I cannot find the words in English—or in my own language—to describe the suffering we went through," said Youk Chhang, who survived the killing fields himself but lost his brother and sister in them. By the time the Khmer Rouge was overthrown in 1979, Cambodia was completely devastated. Lives and families were broken, cities and infrastructure were destroyed, social and political institutions were corrupted, and the economy was bankrupt.

Cambodian Youth Fighters

Theravada Buddhism has been the national religion of Cambodia since the thirteenth century, except during the reign of the Khmer Rouge from 1975 to 1979. Historically, there have been very few Christians in Cambodia. "Cambodian Communities out of Crisis," a Christian charity active in Cambodia, estimates that the Christian population in Cambodia reached ten thousand people in 1975, but during the rule of the Khmer Rouge that number was reduced to just two hundred.[72] Then, in 1990, when the church was granted freedom by the government to function openly, there were about ten evangelical churches in the country.[73] According to Joshua Project, 3.4 percent of the population now profess to be Christians, with evangelicals representing more than half of that number. It is encouraging to note that the evangelical growth rate is 8.8 percent per year.[74]

---

72   "The Christian Church in Cambodia," Cambodian Communities out of Crisis, http://cambcomm.org.uk/ccc/the-christian-church-in-cambodia/.

73   Ibid.

74   "People Groups: Cambodia," Joshua Project, https://joshuaproject.net/countries/CB.

The post–Khmer Rouge era in Cambodia has proven to be a huge window of opportunity for the advance of the gospel as never seen before in the history of that nation.

In 1998 I was invited to Cambodia to help facilitate the first CHE training. By 2007 about a dozen ministries were using the strategy in eighty-nine communities and seven provinces. More about that later.

Before we move on, it's important to know a little more about the religious context in the country. While the majority of people in Cambodia claim to be Buddhists, their Buddhism is often a glossy covering over deeper animistic beliefs. Buddhism denies the existence of a personal God and leaves man entirely on his own in his struggle for freedom from sin and suffering. As part of their struggle, Cambodians seek to please and appease the spirits which are perceived to control the circumstances of their lives. They live in constant fear of offending these spirits, and consequently structure their lives with rituals that are intended to placate them. As a result, they worship idols and a host of created things.

One of the Cambodian people's greatest felt needs is deliverance from the fear of evil spirits. Cambodian believers described one of the many rituals used in their villages to ward off evil spirits. In the unfortunate event of a stillborn birth, the bodies of these tiny babies are roasted over a fire, wrapped in strips of cloth, and then placed in their homes to ward off disease.

One experience I had in Battambang, Cambodia, brought home to me the need to proclaim salvation through faith in Christ that not only brings forgiveness and eternal life but also deliverance from the powers of darkness. I was in Battambang for a week to train a group of Khmer believers in CHE. Early in the morning, before our seminar would begin each day, I went jogging with Jay Bell, the Asia coordinator for Grace Brethren International Mission.

Having just gained our stride for a jog of about three miles, Jay and I heard a horrifying sound, one that has yet to fade from my memory. Turning quickly to the right toward the source of the screams, we saw a raging young woman with half of a brick in each hand. Her eyes were bulging, her face was distorted, and she was screaming words we couldn't understand.

Jay recognized immediately what was going on. He turned toward the woman, held out his hand, and said softly, "All authority in heaven and earth has been given to Jesus, and he is here." Her face immediately calmed, and she quit yelling. Her arms dropped to her side, the bricks no longer a threatening weapon. The two of us walked toward her, hands outstretched, continuing to call upon the name of Jesus. When we reached the woman, she gave me the bricks that were in her hands. We couldn't speak her language, and she couldn't speak ours. After a few moments, she turned away and walked back the same way she had come.

Then we noticed a crowd of perhaps fifty young men, students from a dormitory at the nearby teachers' college, gathered across the street. Several of them had towels around their waists because they had rushed out from their baths. We asked them if they knew the woman who had been screaming. They could only say, repeatedly, "She is crazy." Someone managed to volunteer in broken English: "She is suffering from disappointment because she has been raped by multiple men." She was recognized in the community as someone who was crazy, dangerous, and deeply disturbed.

Jay and I decided to continue our jog, turning to go in the opposite direction the woman took. And we prayed. While we ran for the next mile or two, we prayed out loud for the woman's conversion. We asked God to make the bricks she had left behind, and that we still held in our hands as we jogged, a memorial to his power in the town of Battambang.

As we were nearing our hotel, we saw the woman again, now standing alone in the street, just a few yards from the police station. We asked a nearby officer to tell the woman that we wanted to take her to our hotel restaurant to get something to eat. The officer told us that the woman's name was Ta Hua; and to our amazement, she agreed to come.

Ta Hua (center) and team

Jay then went to call Perri Snyder, a married woman who had come with her husband as part of the Grace Brethren team and was also staying in our hotel. Jay and Perrit treated Ta Hua to breakfast, after which they went back outside and chatted calmly for about an hour until it was time to leave for our seminar that day. As we climbed onto our motorcycles, the two women embraced, and Ta Hua quietly walked away.

Jay and I were reminded of the story of the demoniac in the region of the Gerasenes as told in the Gospel of Mark. He was possessed by a whole legion of demons when Jesus arrived and drove them out. Likewise, Jesus was in Battambang that morning to release Ta Hua from the grip of dark spiritual forces. I see no other explanation for what happened. At the mention of Jesus' name Ta Hua's face calmed, and her disposition instantly changed.

Paul's letter to the Colossians states that Jesus accomplished two things by the cross: He forgave us of all our sins (2:13–14), and he disarmed the powers and authorities, making a public spectacle of them (2:15). In the West, we like to focus on the first great accomplishment—the forgiveness of sins. However, we shouldn't neglect the second. Satan and his armies have been disarmed! Jesus "has rescued us from the dominion of darkness and brought us into the kingdom of the Son he loves" (Col 1:13)!

> Wholistic ministry that addresses both physical and spiritual poverty will not only play a role in rehabilitating the victims of trafficking, but also in empowering and protecting those most vulnerable to exploitation.

> Wholistic ministry recognizes the battle that rages in the spirit world for the souls of people and the victory that has been accomplished by Christ's death and resurrection.

Trafficking and prostitution are also big problems in Cambodia. A Khmer saying speaks to the double standard in society for men and women: "Men are like gold—if you drop them in the dirt you can pick them up and dust them off. But women are like cloth—if you drop them in the dirt they are soiled forever." Girls caught up in prostitution in Cambodia are considered dirty and irredeemable.

One of the participants in a training I did in Cambodia, her name was Gudron, worked for a charitable organization that had established a home for the rehabilitation of young prostitutes in Phnom Penh. The girls would stay in this home for eighteen months, being cared for physically, emotionally, and spiritually. They would receive teaching from God's Word and were taught a trade skill that they could use to make a living when they eventually returned to their villages. At the end of each young woman's time at the rehabilitation home, a member of the staff would accompany her back to her village to ensure that she would be able to become established and earn sufficient money with the skills she had learned.

Gudron came to the training we were hosting to explore the possibility of including CHE as part of the curriculum in this home. By including CHE principles, the girls would be better equipped to live healthier lives and even become health promoters and evangelists in their respective villages.

There is a direct link between human trafficking, prostitution, and poverty in Southeast Asia. The most vulnerable girls come from the hill tribes or poor villages in the plains, where they live without access to clean water, electricity, medical care, or education. Parents who are crushed and overwhelmed by the burdens and hardship of extreme poverty often sell their young daughters into slavery. Recruiters prey on these families, persuading and bribing the parents to sell their daughters, or sometimes even outright kidnapping the girls.[75] Wholistic ministry that addresses both physical and spiritual poverty will not only play a role in rehabilitating the victims of trafficking, but also in empowering and protecting those most vulnerable to exploitation.

Wholistic ministry recognizes the battle that rages in the spirit world for the souls of people and the victory that has been accomplished by Christ's death and resurrection.

---

[75] Sex Trafficking and Prostitution, *Connections to Poverty* (2008), https://stanford.edu/group/womenscourage/cgi-bin/blogs/sextraffickingandprostitution/tag/poverty-and-sex-trafficking/.

Kampong Speu and Khien Svay

In 1998, Diane Campbell introduced CHE as a strategy to the Assemblies of God. She invited me to come to Cambodia along with my mentor, Stan Rowland. She helped arrange the first CHE training in Cambodia for a group of her colleagues and went on to work with nationals to establish the first CHE ministries. Diane was concerned with the living conditions in the villages she served and wanted a strategy that responded to both the physical and the spiritual needs of the people.

It didn't take Diane long to note that many of the children in the villages had swollen bellies, caused by worms. Diane also passed by stagnant ponds lined with floating trash, recognizing this as the perfect breeding grounds for the mosquitoes that carry malaria and dengue fever. Her research told her that mothers spent an average of 60 percent of their income on medicines for their sick children, and as a consequence they were not able to come up with enough money to keep their children in school. Diane observed firsthand the amulets and rituals used to ward off the evil spirits that were believed to be the source of sickness and disease. She desperately wanted to see these villagers lifted out of extreme poverty and brought to faith in Christ.[76]

The CHE work of the Assemblies of God in Cambodia was funded initially by Fida International, a mission agency of the Pentecostal Churches of Finland, and Action Missionnaire, a mission agency of the French Assemblies of God. Two years after the initiation of CHE work, Fida published a midterm evaluation of the work they had overseen. CHE work had already expanded into forty-eight villages, more than five hundred volunteers had been mobilized, and the lives of over ten thousand families had been impacted.

The evaluation itself focused on just five of the forty-eight villages. Four of the five communities were in the province of Kampong Speu, and the other was in Khien Svay. Here are some highlights from the published report:[77]

- One in three heads of household in the Kampong Speu villages, and one in ten in Khien Svay, had opened their hearts to the Lord and had been baptized.

- There were half the number of cases of typhoid, intestinal parasites, and fever as there had been at the beginning of the program.

- The incidences of diarrhea in children less than five years old had been cut to just one quarter of the number when the program began three years earlier. (Cambodia had at the time, and still has today, the highest infant and under-five mortality rates in the region, and diarrhea has been a primary cause.)[78]

---

76 From Diane Campbell's newsletter, January 2000.

77 Bruno Feuillerat, "AOG Mid Term Review Survey Report: Community Health Education Program," Assemblies of God—Cambodia, 2003.

78 "Cambodia," UNICEF, https://www.unicef.org/infobycountry/cambodia_2190.html.

- Medical expenses for individual families had been reduced between 10 and 50 percent.
- Participating families experienced agricultural and animal productions two times more diversified than that of nonparticipating families.

Numbers and statistics are inadequate to tell the whole story. Bruno Feuillerat, CHE program manager from 1999 to 2005, reported that the Holy Spirit was moving mightily in CHE villages through visions, divine healing, and sincere conversions.

In February of 2004, I received the following written testimony from Saen Sokh Luen, a fifteen-year-old girl in Kompong Speu. Her father had been killed in a road accident, and her mother worked tirelessly to provide for her, along with her three sisters and two brothers. Saen's mom farmed rice and bought chickens in the village and sold them in the market. She worked the fields, sunrise to sunset, barely making enough to get by. Day after day she faced the blistering heat with a well-worn sickle, bare feet on brown earth, and a large straw hat to shade her from the raging sun. It was backbreaking labor—that only earned pennies.

For two years, Saen participated with four of her siblings in CHE meetings in her village, but her mother was too busy to attend. Saen learned about sanitation and hygiene, and about how to prevent malaria, dengue fever, and HIV/AIDs. She studied moral values, such as love and forgiveness, and learned about Jesus.

Saen saw improvements in her village as a result of the CHE program. The house next door had a well, and the families in her neighborhood had latrines and water filters in their homes. Families were loaned a sow and a new variety of rice seeds, which didn't have to be paid back until the sow had piglets and the rice seeds produced a harvest. Here's how Saen told more of the story:

> Thanks to the Lord, our harvest this year was greater by 30 percent. Our circumstances have improved and our standard of living increased. Our health is better. Before we often had "the typhoid" and spent much on medical care. We are now seldom sick. There is a better environment at our house because several of us know Jesus. There is more love, more mutual respect, and lies and slander have disappeared. The situation has also changed in the village because many of my neighbors have also come to follow Christ. I am happy to know Jesus, and now share this good news in the village and at school. My friends are also converted.
>
> Several times Jesus answered my prayers. I requested to succeed at my examinations at school, and I succeeded! I prayed for my friend who was very sick in spite of medical treatment, and she was cured! I prayed for my seventy-year-old grandfather who was forgetting our names and could not recognize his close relations, and he remembers us again. I prayed for enough money to go to school, and the Lord blessed our income. I can go to school!

Saen is not just telling her story, but the story of thousands of others touched by the wholistic work of Christians from many different churches and organizations throughout Cambodia. Lives and communities are being transformed as people give their hearts to the Lord and become followers of Jesus.

Rapid Multiplication

Tun Chhay a Cambodian pastor, joined the CHE leadership team of the Assemblies of God in 2002, serving alongside of Diane Campbell, Bruno Feuillerat, and John Cottrell, the director of the Assemblies of God mission in Cambodia. In 2004 they formed Cambodia Global Action (CGA), a national NGO. Pastor Chhay became the first director of CGA, and served in that role from 2004 to 2017.

Pastor Chhay recognized CHE as a tool for building up the existing church as well as for planting new ones. He saw that CHE was planting churches three times faster than everything else the Assemblies of God had done combined. During his tenure, 90 percent of all Assemblies of God pastors in the country were trained in CHE, and the strategy was adopted by the national church.

As other organizations in the country picked up on the strategy, Pastor Chhay facilitated a CHE working group in Cambodia, which brought different organizations together for the strengthening of individual ministries and the greater expansion of the movement. In collaboration, they shared information, worked together on the translation of CHE lesson plans from English to Khmer, and developed a strategy for reaching the nation. This would eventually become a pattern around the world: national coalitions with national strategies.

By 2007, there were a dozen or so different organizations using the CHE strategy in the country, including CGA and the Assemblies of God, Christian Missionary Alliance, Samaritan's Purse, Holistic Community Development Initiatives, Asian Outreach, Neighbors of Cambodia, Evangelical Fellowship of Cambodia, Fida International, Food for the Hungry International, and Medical Ambassadors International. Collectively, they had worked in eighty-nine villages spread throughout seven provinces.

The Assemblies of God, through their local NGO, Cambodia Global Action, had the largest outreach, with

> As other organizations in the country picked up on the strategy, Pastor Chhay facilitated a CHE working group in Cambodia, bringing different organizations together for the strengthening of individual ministries and the expansion of the movement. They shared information, worked together on the translation of CHE lessons, and developed a strategy for reaching the nation. This would eventually become a pattern around the world: national coalitions with national strategies.

557 volunteer committee members and 1,344 CHEs in seventy-six villages. They planted eight churches, and they had an additional sixty-one cell groups, with 1,425 new believers, on the road to becoming churches. Not only was the church growing, but communities were developing. The government of Cambodia was so impressed with CHE that they not only sanctioned the work in the country but made the CHE committees official government entities. That meant that electing a CHE committee in Cambodia's villages involved ballots, a ballot box, and an election watch!

On a recent trip to Cambodia, I interviewed Pastor Chhay and his colleague, Sothou Ken, who served with him as a master trainer while at CGA. They reported that CHE has continued strong in Cambodia for twenty years (1998 to 2018). During their tenure with CGA, they established CHE ministries in 227 different villages. As communities developed and churches were established, communities became self-sustaining and CGA trainers moved on to new communities.

As of 2018, CGA had a CHE department with four master training teams coordinating the CHE work in forty new villages. Pastor Chhay and Sothou were working out of their local church in thirteen communities in northern Cambodia. In partnership with World Challenge, they were pressing toward their goal of transforming seventy-five communities and planting seventy-five churches within four years. They also reported that there were an additional thirty active church-based programs within the Assemblies of God. And in recent years, significant works have been initiated with TransWorld Radio, the Christian Reformed Church, the Presbyterian Church, and a group of independent churches. Moving on from Cambodia, our next stop in Southeast Asia is Indonesia.

Indonesia: Muslims Are Not "Allergic" to Christians Anymore

Indonesia, with 265 million people, is the fourth-most populous country in the world, after China, India, and the United States. It has the largest Muslim population, comprising 12.6 percent of the world's Muslims, followed by India (11.1 percent), and Pakistan (10.5 percent).[79]

Indonesia is a cluster of more than eighteen thousand islands, making it the largest archipelago in the world.[80] According to Joshua Project, there are 784 people groups living on these islands, with 231 of them being classified as unreached. These 231 people groups represent 62.8% of that nation's population, or 166 million people.

---

79 "The Countries with the 10 Largest Christian Populations and the 10 Largest Muslim Populations," Pew Research Center, April 1, 2019, https://www.pewresearch.org/fact-tank/2019/04/01/the-countries-with-the-10-largest-christian-populations-and-the-10-largest-muslim-populations/.

80 Amber Pariona, "How Many Islands Are There in Indonesia?" WorldAtlas, February 19, 2018, https://www.worldatlas.com/articles/how-many-islands-does-indonesia-have.html.

The island of Java contains more than half of the nation's population and dominates the rest of the country politically and economically.[81] Jakarta, the capital city of Indonesia, is located in Western Java.

My first experience in Jakarta was in 1998, when Far East Broadcasting Company (FEBC), Indonesia, invited me to conduct a three-day CHE vision seminar with leaders from various Christian ministries around the country. Later that same year, in an informal setting with Samuel Tritamihardja, an engineer and the director of the organization, a vision for reaching the least and the lost was birthed. Samuel suggested that workers on the ground could be mobilized to teach health topics among target peoples. With that, he would put together corresponding radio broadcasts to reinforce what was being taught by word of mouth. In this way, it was dreamed that "radio churches" would assemble, being made up of people who came to Christ by listening to the radio and who desired to gather regularly in listening groups for worship. Samuel proposed that CHE could be the "ground force," and he would be the "air force."

Indonesian Farmer

As the training events organized by FEBC got going, their public relations officer, Ibu Rebecca Kistap, proved invaluable. This talented woman not only hosted the events, invited the participants, and managed the logistics, but she also served as my interpreter for much of the time I was in Jakarta. At one point, Rebecca came to me and said that God had laid it on her heart to resign from FEBC Indonesia in order to serve as a country facilitator for CHE. She did just that, and served for more than fifteen years, training and equipping groups of believers from different churches and ministries. By 2013 she had established CHE ministries in forty-three different communities and was working in partnership with eighteen different faith-based organizations or church denominations on seven different islands.[82]

Rebecca retired as CHE Coordinator in 2015 and began teaching wholistic ministry at "The Diamonds of the Nation" seminary in Jakarta the following year. She developed online and offline classes for both undergraduate and graduate

---

81 "Java," Encyclopedia Britannica, https://www.britannica.com/place/Java-island-Indonesia.
82 From an activity report written by Rebecca Kistap in 2013.

degree programs. She has also produced two hundred radio scripts from CHE lesson plans in cooperation with YASKI, Radio Sentosa, and TransWorld Radio at Batu-Malang. These programs continue to be broadcast in the Sundanese, Minangnese, and Javanese languages.

The stories that follow represent a short history of the early beginnings of CHE work in Indonesia under Rebecca's leadership.

Success at a Price

The first CHE program in Indonesia was implemented in South Sumatra among an unreached people group there. Panuta (not his real name), the first active Indonesian CHE trainer, courageously planted five churches in Muslim areas, but not without great endurance and extreme hardship. Each of his churches, at one time or another, were burned, and his congregations experienced periodic persecution.

> By 2013, Rebecca had established CHE ministries in forty-three different communities and was working in partnership with eighteen different faith-based organizations or church denominations on seven different islands in Indonesia.

When I visited Sumatra for the first time in February of 1999, the volunteer CHE workers there told stories of mobs regularly raiding the nearby police station to abduct and kill some of the prisoners. The people judged matters for themselves because they don't trust the police and the courts to deliver justice appropriately. One unfortunate prisoner who was kidnapped and murdered had done no more than steal rubber from a neighbor's tree. My hosts showed me a house that had been gutted by fire and was the site where six men received "punishment" for stealing a cow—one of them had been disemboweled; another's head had been flattened with a beam. Tensions were always flaring between the two major Muslim groups in the area, to the point that a recent riot resulted in the town market being burned and three people from each group being killed.

Panuta, a dedicated man of God, had a good reputation in the community. One Muslim man I spoke with volunteered, "If Muslims ever come after Pastor Panuta, I will be the first one to fight to defend him. He is a good man."

In the midst of such turmoil, Panuta's testimony is especially moving. His father, a devout Muslim, had built a mosque in their hometown; and as a boy, Panuta often called the community to prayer at the five designated times each day. Encouraged by his family, the young Muslim would also sing the Koran over the loudspeaker on these occasions.

During his youth, Panuta got involved with the Javanese occult. He gained impressive mystical powers—people couldn't harm him with a knife; he could drink excessively without getting drunk; women were especially attracted to him. He admits that he didn't use the attraction spells often, though, because part of the magic required that he couldn't touch the affected woman. But despite the fact that Panuta had much power, he didn't have any peace. Then he heard that Christ is the Prince of Peace.

Wanting to know more, Panuta started to investigate. He attended mass at a Catholic church on two occasions, but he decided against becoming Catholic because he noticed the presence of idols in the cathedral, and Islam teaches that those who pray to idols will go to hell. Next, Panuta visited an evangelical church. However, since most of the members were Chinese, he didn't want to join that group either. Another reason why Panuta didn't want to return to that church was because the preacher wore a black robe, resembling the one worn by his Javanese occult teacher.

> Despite the fact that Panuta had much power, he did not have any peace. Then, he heard that Christ was the Prince of Peace.

About this time, Panuta's brother, Pramana (also not his real name), had a problem that forced him to leave home. Volunteering to accompany Pramana to Jakarta by train, the two young men headed to the capital city. They couldn't find seats for the long ride, so they slept on the floor, covering it with newspapers. Upon arriving in Jakarta, they saw an ad in one of the newspapers on which they slept about a revival meeting in Jakarta, and they decided to attend.

Panuta and Pramana entered the stadium and sat at the back, high up in the "H" section. When the speaker that night challenged and urged the audience to make a commitment to follow Jesus, many people ran to the front. Panuta felt someone pulling him to go forward, but he couldn't see anyone grasping his arm or hand. He resisted at first, but then mentioned it to his brother. They discussed what a decision to become a Christian would mean; and together, they decided to accept the call. Today they are both pastors.

After attending a vision seminar that I facilitated in Jakarta in April of 1998, Panuta was convinced CHE would open new opportunities among the poor Muslim farmers in his area of Indonesia. I returned in July of that same year and conducted the first Training of Trainers (TOT) and then returned yet two more times to teach TOT 2 and TOT 3. I taught ninety-three CHE class hours in Jakarta, and Panuta attended almost every session. After completing the first phase of our training, Panuta recruited seventeen workers and trained them for ministry in six different villages.

I wanted to see firsthand some of what Panuta and his team were doing, so in April of 1999 I boarded a small plane in Jakarta bound for South Sumatra, where Panuta worked. He was serving among an unreached people group of almost two million. As the engines began to turn, something like smoke filled the cabin! It turned out to be a harmless mist from the plane's air conditioner. I did wonder how well the plane had been maintained. A fellow passenger explained it to me, "Every time we fly here, the clouds come inside!"

We made it safely to our destination and Panuta took me to meet some of the area farmers with whom he had been working. These Muslim men were being trained using lessons from our open-source CHE curriculum and had been experiencing high levels of success. The demonstration farm appeared to be so well developed that I was sure they had been working it for years. To my surprise, they had only begun nine months before, after the CHE training in July! There were fishponds, rice paddies, vegetable gardens, and fruit trees. They were also manufacturing roofing tiles as a method of income generation.

> Panuta took me to the door of the building and repeated the words "No eating! No eating!"
> Our interpreter explained that the building was a house of prayer and fasting where Panuta asks for God's blessing on the farm.

In the middle of the farm was a small building made with bamboo siding and covered with a tile roof. Panuta took me to the door of the building and repeated the words "No eating! No eating!" as he waved his hand back and forth in the air. Our interpreter (who was already worn out at this point from having to interpret so much of our conversations) explained that the building was a house of prayer and fasting where Panuta asks for God's blessing on the farm. Panuta loves to share about this place and is also quick to point out the building to the Muslim farmers who come to learn from what he is doing, telling them the key to his success is praying to God in Jesus' name!

In a brief meeting with Panuta and his team, they listed on a blackboard a number of successes related to the impact of their work with area Muslims. As each item was shared, and then interpreted into English for my benefit, I made note of it.

- CHE is proving to be a tool for working hand in hand with the community.
- People in the community have seen progress and are hopeful and enthusiastic about their future.
- There is unity in the community. Trainers, committee members, and CHEs are working together with a common vision.
- People in the community are healthier. They are eating right, and they seldom get sick.
- Two training centers have been built.
- The environment is cleaner, and the CHEs are gaining the respect and admiration of others.
- The CHEs are succeeding with income generation. They are cultivating their land, selling vegetables, and raising chickens. They are planning for a cooperative to produce cassava chips and make tiles for roofs. As one man put it, "I have a better home. I used to live in a very small house in the forest."

- Muslims are not "allergic" to Christians anymore. Because of the CHE program, Muslims value and respect the CHEs as Christians and are working together with them.
- People are becoming aware of their spiritual condition and learning from the Bible. Their thinking and character are changing. They are learning right from wrong and moving in a new direction.

> God was breaking down the walls of hostility between Christians and Muslims, and people in the community were working together for the common good.

God was breaking down walls of hostility between Christians and Muslims, and people in the community were working together for the common good.

A Long, Hard Struggle

Many other stories could be told about CHE in Indonesia. I am going to share just one more because it illustrates the kind of commitment and dedication required to establish a presence among the unreached of that country. The twenty-two million Sundanese of Indonesia comprise one of the largest groups of people yet unreached for Christ. They don't know or understand Christian ideals, and they have been led to believe Christians are dirty people who treat Muslims like dogs. That is why Muslims from this people group will wipe off a chair that was just vacated by a Christian before sitting in it themselves.

In order to reach people who have been taught to think this way, Christians must live as Christ among them and let them see the love and character of a true follower of Christ. A businessman named Silas (not his real name) responded to this call to be Christ among the Sundanese and to establish a church among them. He bought a home and set up a business in their community. When asked about his commitment, Silas simply says, "I am ready to die."

Using CHE principles as the framework for his ministry, Silas purposefully lived among the Sundanese to help them overcome their prejudices. He used his business to enrich the lives of people in that community rather than for his own personal financial gain. He provided jobs for locals, taught those around him how to prevent disease with good sanitation and hygiene, and helped his Muslim friends grow gardens and raise animals for food. He also taught moral values from the Scriptures, which, in turn, helped everyone build strong families and a stable community. Silas was letting his light shine in the darkness, developing relationships and building bridges that would one day allow those blinded by prejudice to see the truth about Jesus and his followers.

Islam has been called the Mount Everest of Christian mission, meaning it is a long and difficult journey to reach this population for Christ. Silas, like many others, embarked on that journey. Being the largest Muslim country in the world, it will be an uphill trek to take the gospel to the remaining unreached in Indonesia. It will require many more dedicated workers like Silas who are willing to climb the mountain using a wholistic strategy and who are ready to die for the cause of Christ. Catalyzing transformational movements sometimes requires great sacrifice.

Vietnam: Miracles, Faith, and Community Transformation

The Socialist Republic of Vietnam, located on the eastern side of the Indochina Peninsula in Southeast Asia, is home to more than ninety-seven million people. The Joshua Project identifies 118 people groups in the country, 67 of which are classified as unreached as of 2020. Over half (51.3 percent) profess to be Buddhist and 10.2 percent claim to be Christian.[83] It is worth noting that a significant majority of Protestants/evangelicals are from the nation's ethnic minority groups. The Hmong have been particularly responsive.[84]

The church in Vietnam has grown amid considerable persecution. Christians have been viewed to be counter-revolutionary and a possible threat to the Communist authorities. Pastors and lay people, especially those from minority groups and unregistered house churches, have been imprisoned. Government restrictions are most severe in the north. According to research by Overseas Missionary Fellowship (OMF), there are currently only about fifteen registered churches in the north, although hundreds of minority congregations are awaiting registration. In the capital city of Hanoi, there is only one registered church. In the south of the country, where there are fewer restrictions, there are more than one thousand registered churches and meeting places, including more than fifty in Ho Chi Minh City (formerly Saigon).[85]

During my first visit to Vietnam, I recall sitting on the floor in a small room in a secret place—out of view of the police—where pastors often meet for training. Our meal was spread out on the floor in the midst of our tiny circle. My interpreter, Linh (not her real name), sat to my right. She looked at me and said, "They are talking now about a pastor who died in prison."

"Was he mistreated, or did he die of natural causes?" I asked.

"He was mistreated."

"Recently?" I inquired.

"No, some time ago."

"Are any of your pastors in prison today?"

"Just one," she replied, and then she proceeded to tell me his story.

---

83 "People Groups: Vietnam," Joshua Project, https://joshuaproject.net/countries/VM.
84 "About Vietnam," OMF International, https://omf.org/asia/vietnam/about-vietnam/.
85 Ibid.

Pastor Binh (not his real name) lives and works in a part of Vietnam where Christians suffer the most intense persecution. He is twenty-eight years old, and he and his wife have six children. His wife survives by farming a small plot of land. Binh was first imprisoned in 1994 for doing pastoral work. After two years he was released, but just a year later he was caught again, this time teaching basic doctrine to a new convert. The young believer, fearing imprisonment himself, testified against Binh, who received a sentence of three years this time. Three years in prison for teaching basic doctrine to one new convert!

> By 2006 these churches were experiencing explosive growth. They reported 47 CHE programs impacting 205 villages. CHE was "a revolutionary concept to many Vietnamese churches after a long time concentrating on meeting just the spiritual needs of people."

I was brought into Vietnam through connections with Far East Broadcasting Company and Open Doors. Pastor Vic Mendoza, the director of CHE work in the Philippines, accompanied me to help with training. Our assignment was to train national pastors from the underground church for CHE ministry in villages throughout the central highlands. Between 1998 and 2000, Vic and I returned either together or individually several times in order to train house church pastors in CHE and to consult with house church leaders.

Although these trips could be considered somewhat routine, they were always filled with risk and adventure. My hosts would instruct me to go to my hotel and wait for a phone call. When I received the call, I would be told where to go to find a vehicle that had been sent to pick me up. From that point, I would be taken to a windowless room prepared for our gathering. The driver never joined me but would only drop me off at the facility and point to the room. I would then sit there alone and wait as pastors came in one at a time. We would stay huddled on the floor together the whole day—singing, praying, and discussing the principles and methods of CHE.

A Movement in the Central Highlands

Initially, the growth of CHE in the central highlands of Vietnam was explosive, as house churches embraced the concept and equipped their missionaries and house church pastors. By the end of the year 2000, 105 family-based CHEs were serving forty-seven villages and nine different ethnic groups; 918 people had made professions of faith; and community volunteers had built eighty-eight latrines, 125 rubbish pits, and twelve new water sources.[86]

The underground work with house churches continued, and its management was turned over to a medical doctor and surgeon (I will refer to him as Josh) who ventured as a missionary to Vietnam from the Philippines. Josh dedicated his life

---
86 From internal reports submitted to Medical Ambassadors.

to a ministry of outreach to people living under the oppression of communist governments. Police read his email, placed a tap on his phone, and tracked his movements. Nevertheless, Josh continued to provide training to equip believers for ministry and outreach. When he left home each day, he was uncertain where that day's training would take place. Referring to a list of four addresses that had been passed along to him, Josh would methodically make his way from place to place, searching for the eager learners. If nobody was at the first address, he would go to the second, and then the third, and then the fourth—until he found the group! For many years, Josh struggled to find effective means for outreach in such hostile circumstances. Then he learned CHE.

Pastor Vic, director of CHE in the Philippines, made several trips to encourage the workers in the central highlands. On one of his trips, he traveled about two hours by bus from Ho Chi Minh City and then walked another three to four miles uphill on rough terrain to a village where he met with several house church evangelists. The evangelists told of wells being dug and of water being filtered and boiled with methods they had learned from previous encounters with us in the secret closed-door CHE training seminars near the seashore. They told of latrines being made by village folks. With joyful hearts, they testified about people coming to the Lord—in some areas by the hundreds!

Two evangelists told of miracles God had done in the villages. One of the events took place in the home where they were meeting. The owner of the house, DT, had gone blind. Both his wife and daughter were also going blind. As a result of his blindness, DT could no longer work. As a result, the family was suffering from extreme poverty. But when DT and his household received Christ as their Lord and Savior, they were healed of their blindness! With their sight restored, they were able to repair their home, making it not only fit as a dwelling but also improving it so it could be used for area church meetings and CHE training and gatherings. DT and his family welcomed everyone without fear that the police or soldiers would arrest them for offering their home as a Christian meeting place. Because of this witness, most of DT's relatives likewise came to the Lord.

The other evangelist told about a miracle that happened during CHE training in another village. A two-year-old toddler fell on her face in a mud puddle. No one saw her fall, but when she was discovered her mouth and nose were filled with mud and she was no longer breathing. The evangelists and all the Christians in the village started praying for the little girl, and shortly thereafter she started to move and breathe. The following morning, liquid mud started flowing out of the girl's nose and mouth. Later that day she was running and playing as if nothing had happened to her. This miraculous event brought almost all the villagers to Christ.

After coming out of the central highlands, Pastor Vic testified, "All the time I was with these workers of Christ—working among the poorest people in these mountains, I felt so small and so humble before the Lord. My heart seemed to burst with joy and praise to the Lord for the wonderful things he was doing in these tribal areas."[87]

Unfortunately, it was difficult to multiply trainers in the highlands, and while the initial results remained, the movement died out.

A Second Movement Catalyzed

Soon after Josh began his work with house churches in 1997, he, along with a Vietnamese medical doctor I will refer to as Danh, also began teaching CHE to a large group of churches in the country. At the end of 2005, Josh wrote to me, excited about a most fruitful year of ministry. He had conducted CHE training weekly "without letup," and the result was twelve CHE training teams in twelve provinces partnering with thirty-one churches and ministering in seventy-one villages with approximately 150,000 residents. As the consequences of twenty thousand homes receiving visits from CHEs, nine hundred families became followers of Jesus; six new churches were planted; thirty-five deep wells were drilled, 189 water filters were made; 435 latrines were constructed; and more than six hundred families were working on developing microbusinesses.[88]

By 2006 these churches were experiencing explosive growth. They reported forty-seven CHE programs impacting 205 villages. CHE volunteers shared the good news 13,072 times, and 1,390 people made professions of faith and were being discipled into the church. Leaders in Vietnam testified that churches using CHE had become agents of transformation in their communities—facilitating improvements in sanitation, hygiene, water purification, home gardening, animal husbandry, agriculture, and small businesses. They were working with communities to fix roads, clean up the environment, and provide more permanent shelters. CHE churches were recognized for initiating social awareness campaigns to fight drug addiction, gambling, prostitution, child abuse, and domestic violence—as well as working toward the empowerment of women.

One of the national leaders of the CHE program in Vietnam stated that CHE was "a revolutionary concept to many Vietnamese churches after a long time concentrating on meeting just the spiritual needs of the people. Now it has brought a new method to the church."[89]

When I returned to Vietnam in 2018, the religious and political climate was very different than it was more than it was twenty years ago when I first visited the country. Many churches, especially in the south, now have registration papers and are officially recognized by the government. Churches across the nation are gaining recognition for the positive contributions they are making to Vietnamese society.

---

87 Vic Mendoza, Internal Monitoring and Report Summaries, Medical Ambassadors, Modesto, CA, 2002.
88 Dr. J, Internal Monitoring and Report Summaries, Medical Ambassadors, Modesto, CA, 2005.
89 My newsletters to supporters.

Myanmar: A New Way of Doing Ministry

Young Buddhist in Myanmar

Myanmar, formerly known as Burma, is a Buddhist country on the northeast shores of the Bay of Bengal. It is bordered by India and Bangladesh to the west, China to the north, and Laos and Thailand to the east. Myanmar has had a long history of coups, wars, and rebellions. When I first traveled to Myanmar in 1998, the Burmese military maintained forcible control over the country. Universities in the city of Yangon had been closed for eight years to prevent student uprisings.

Despite the prohibition at the time against missionaries entering Myanmar, the Assemblies of God has had a historical and considerable presence in the country, with more than 1,350 local churches and 350,000 members.[90] In 1998, I was invited by Fida International, as a guest facilitator, to help introduce the CHE strategy to the local church leadership. Our vision seminar for about forty-five pastors was met with enthusiastic response. I returned several times over the next few years to train and consult.

During my first visit to Myanmar in 1998, I met Pastor U Myo Chit—a sixth-generation believer in the line of the missionary statesman Adoniram Judson (1788–1850). He was the general secretary for the Assemblies of God in the country. Myo Chit was a jovial man who liked to have fun. Before I preached as a guest speaker at his church, Myo Chit told me to put on a *longgi*, a wrap-around skirt which men wear in that part of the world. Then he said, "Jump up and down three times shouting 'Hallelujah!' If you can do this without the *longgi* falling off, then I will permit you to address the people!"

My trips into Myanmar were always memorable, and sometimes frightening. On my second or third trip, I was training a group of pastors to start CHE ministries in their communities. During a break, I went up on the platform to tape notes onto the wall from our dialogue that day, which had been scribed poster paper. Below the platform, Myo Chit maintained a radio studio where he recorded and broadcast programs on the FEBC network. As I stretched to tape the paper to the wall, I accidentally stepped sideways into a stairwell leading down to the studio. There were no guard rails around the cavity that was the entrance to a stairway that went down almost two floors. There was nothing to stop me from falling approximately twelve feet onto the last of concrete steps at the bottom of the well.

---

90 Taken from an internal document by Fida International that was partnering with the Assemblies of God at the time.

I remember the fall as if it happened in slow motion, thinking as I dropped, "I won't survive this. I'm dead." I landed on my back with a painful thud. I got the wind knocked out of me and couldn't breathe. Immediately I heard chatter all around me in Burmese, a language I didn't understand, as the group of pastors from the main floor came down after me. They put their arms under my armpits and around my chest, and as carefully as they could, they started to drag me back up the stairs. I tried—unsuccessfully—to shout to warn them that I shouldn't be moved. I was sure I had broken my back, and that in their effort to move me I would be permanently paralyzed. The men managed to get me upstairs, and then laid me on my stomach on a table in the sanctuary.

The next thing I knew, a man came running toward me from the back of the room, waving his arms and shouting, "Massage! Massage!" Still laying on my stomach, the man grabbed one of my legs and stretched it over my back to the top of my head. I tried again to shout for help, but I couldn't manage to do so.

After what seemed to be a very long time, I caught my breath and was able to breathe normally again. Immediately I shouted for my colleague, Jukka, who was teaching a second group of pastors in another room. Jukka came running and examined my back with his trained medical eye. He said that I had landed on the thickest part of my shoulder blades, so I was fortunately able to endure the blow. If I had landed any other way, the outcome would have likely been quite different.

After Jukka's examination, the pastors gathered around me, thanked God for protecting me from further injury, and prayed for my complete healing. The next day, by God's grace, I was able to resume my teaching. This group of pastors became pioneers for CHE in Myanmar and established a movement that spread rapidly to various parts of the country.

A pilot program was initiated in four communities in Myanmar. The plan was to teach the people to prevent disease and improve the health of the community by training community health volunteers to work with families through home visits. At the same time, a committee was elected and equipped to plan and implement small development projects.

Over the next ten years, hundreds of community projects were completed in various places around the country, and more than one thousand families received microloans from funding provided by Fida International. Some of the projects included watermelon farms, fishponds, rice paddies, vegetable plots using organic fertilizers, and animal husbandry. Many of the people who participated in the initial program became debt-free and looked forward to a better future and improved quality of life.

A few communities were able to buy additional farmland with the proceeds from their projects, which then served to expand their work and further increase their income. Likewise, savings groups were set up in some villages from income generated by the community's projects. The collective savings of groups within the community were used as a sort of insurance to help cover unexpected emergencies. As the benefits of the CHE programs became evident to all those around, the ministry spread from community to community.

In the process of doing this work, churches were strengthened and standing strong because their members had adequate finances to contribute to their sustainability. The entire Assemblies of God denomination in Myanmar embraced a new way of thinking about how to do ministry.

By 2011, the pastors we trained were overseeing a thriving work in sixty-one communities spread throughout eight of the twenty-one administrative divisions of the country. They had trained 631 volunteer committee members and community health evangelists who were owners of the community projects and were making disciples by working with families in their homes to prevent disease, improve living standards, and learn from the Scriptures what it means to follow Jesus.

Papua New Guinea: Released from the Grip of the Powers of Darkness

A villager in Papua New Guinea

With 826 language groups but a total population of only 4.5 million people, Papua New Guinea is the most ethnically and linguistically diverse country on the planet. Though the majority of these people groups have been evangelized, there are still tribes in isolated parts of the country that have yet to be reached. During the early days of church planting in Papua New Guinea, missionaries suffered disease and martyrdom at the hands of cannibals. Nevertheless, they went on to significantly change the nation and its people, as 96 percent of the population now claims to be Christian. Even so, many of the people maintain a nominal and superficial view of their Christianity and have yet to experience a genuine transformation of values and beliefs. The roots of animism are still evident in many aspects of their daily lives.

At the time we approached Papua New Guinea, the government as well as various mission organizations had recognized the need for missionaries with experience in health education and community development. The following statistics describe the needs being faced at that time in the country.

- Fifteen thousand babies less than one year old were dying every year, equaling one out of every ten new births.
- Thirteen thousand children from one to four years old were dying each year, never reaching their fifth birthday.
- Forty-three percent of children of all ages were experiencing malnutrition.
- Fifty percent of all children had not been immunized.
- Seventy percent of rural communities did not have access to safe drinking water.
- 1,610 children were dying each year from diarrhea.[91]

The government of Papua New Guinea recognized that a health promotion of this scale would require grassroots participation. Their plan was to empower individuals, families, and communities to take responsibility for their own health through education programs carried out in cooperation with churches, nongovernment organizations, and the corporate sector. With 96 percent of the population claiming to be Christian, there was at least one church in nearly every village. Government officials acknowledged the church was the *only* institution in the country with the capacity to mobilize the masses. Because much of the country's health services were delivered by the church, even representatives of secular organizations at work in Papua New Guinea admitted they couldn't do what needed to be done without the church. In 2001, the department of health began the implementation of a ten-year program called the "Healthy Islands Initiative."

I went to Papua New Guinea in 2001 with Dr. Bill and Sharon Bieber to explore possibilities for ministry. Bill had served as a provincial health officer in the Eastern Highlands Province and had good relationships with many in the department of health. Since "health" can be defined as a state of complete physical, mental, *spiritual*, and social well-being, we decided to present the ministry of CHE to the national health promotions director and his staff during my visit. By God's grace, they could see the value of such a wholistic approach, and in response invited us to cooperate with them in their Healthy Islands Initiative.

A year after our initial visit with the health promotions director, Bill, Sharon, and I returned to see the progress of the first CHE programs' efforts in the Eastern Highlands. As I was traveling through the mountains, I suddenly became aware that something very significant was taking place. Villages were changing—dramatically! Walkways were decorated with flowers. Families were

---

91 World Health Organization Country Profile: Papua New Guinea.

growing vegetable gardens to provide good nutrition for their children. Homes were ventilated with separate cook houses. People were using latrines. Waste was being disposed of in garbage pits, and dish racks were being used to sanitize dishes in the sun after eating.

This wasn't all that was different, although some of the more significant changes would have likely gone unnoticed by the casual observer. On this return visit, I witnessed people serving one another and cooperating for the good of the community. Pastors had set aside prejudices and joined hands with government workers to meet the needs of those in their villages. Churches from different denominations were uniting in worship and service. People were overcoming the fear of evil spirits and finding the courage to change.

An End to Tribal Warfare

During my second visit to the country, one story of transformation caught my attention. Michael, a tough, rugged government worker and CHE team leader, told me what was happening in Henganofi, a district in the Eastern Highlands. Before Michael and his team started their CHE work, tribes had been at war with one another, some for as long as fifteen years. As a result, schools had been shut down and roads had been barricaded so that government officials and other well-intentioned organizations wouldn't interfere.

A footpath between two previously hostile villages

Tears filled the eyes of many around the table as Michael related how the powers of darkness no longer had their death grip on the villagers' hearts. The tribes were no longer fighting each other; the roadblocks had been removed; and people were working together to beautify their communities. Together they had dug miles of trails into the sides of the mountains—footpaths connecting formerly warring communities. Not only were these paths cut, but they were also fortified with retaining walls built from rocks carried up from the river below and decorated with flowers and plants. What an amazing symbol of reconciliation and indicator of spiritual growth for these communities!

> Pastors had set aside prejudices and joined hands with government workers. Churches from different denominations were uniting in worship and service. People were overcoming the fear of evil spirits and finding the courage to change.

When Michael took us to one of the villages of Henganofi to see these things for ourselves, our CHE team was greeted with fanfare. We were adorned with *leis* (necklaces made of flowers) and *bilums* (handmade crocheted bags that are used to carry goods) and escorted by a throng of dancers.

At the end of the day we were given seats of honor at an assembly in an open field. An elder from the tribe held up a bow and three arrows and announced with great pride, "Our fathers gave us these weapons." Then he took one of the flat-tipped arrows in his right hand and held it up with his left. "This is what we use to kill pigs," he declared. Then the old man showed two arrows with rounded tips. Holding them up, he said, "This is what we used to use to kill people." He put the bow and all the arrows together and handed them to me. "I want to give these to you today," the old man said, "because you have come and taught us a different way of life. You have taught us to live in peace and harmony."

It was humbling to see all that had happened in these villages in just one year. CHE ministries had been initiated in fifty-five different communities in Papua New Guinea, and transformation was spreading like wildfire. Many copycat efforts sprang up once people began to notice the changes taking place in neighboring areas. Encouraged by the unmistakable results they were witnessing, government workers were inspired and invigorated to multiply the successes.

Village chiefs testify to the end of tribal warfare in their valley

CHAPTER 8

Models, Clusters, and Tipping Points

A Million Village Movement

In the introduction to this book, I explained the reasons for the Million Village Challenge. While "one million" is not meant to be an exact number, we can use it as a tool to help define the task and visualize the opportunities facing the church today. By answering the call to engage a million villages, the body of Christ has the unique opportunity to alleviate extreme poverty for the majority of the world's poor and come closer to fulfilling the command of Jesus to take the gospel to the ends of the earth. In order to achieve these goals, however, the global church must come together and be equipped for wholistic community development work in the village.

As believers, our vision goes beyond poverty alleviation and embraces the call of God to take the gospel of the kingdom to every tribe and nation (Matt 24:14). Many of the world's least reached, and a majority of those with no gospel witness among them, live in these million villages. That makes the Million Village Challenge a call we simply cannot ignore.

The Global CHE Network has members all around the world uniquely positioned to train and equip local churches and faith-based organizations for transformational movements among the rural poor. As a network, we are calling the church to join us in this great venture.

> The Global CHE Network has members all around the world uniquely positioned to train and equip the church for catalyzing transformational movements. They invite you to join the movement: www.chenetwork.org

Establishing Model Villages

When a village achieves an active fellowship of believers and success in key areas of community development, such as water, wellness, food security, education, and income generation, that village is potentially a *model*. I say *potentially* because if the change has been owned by outsiders and progress has been delivered to the village in the way of services, we may have only the appearance of a model. Without the underlying fundamentals of self-discovery, local ownership, asset-based development, and integration, what has been achieved by outsiders is likely neither sustainable nor multipliable. Unless it is multipliable, it is not a true model.

> **True model villages are essential to movements. Counterfeit models look good, but they won't multiply.**

True models are established using the principles of transformational movement described in chapter 4 and have changed in ways that are visible to neighboring communities as well as in other ways that are internal and not as obvious. The villagers no longer see themselves as victims or dependents, but as owners of their development processes. Members of the community see a better future for themselves and their neighbors, and they have hope that this vision can be achieved. Leaders and champions in the village are strategically positioned and equipped to lead the community toward the accomplishment of its continuing development. People are taking responsibility for their own health and well-being. The community is united and working together voluntarily for the common good. The community is passing along the change they are experiencing from home to home and village to village.

Where external change has been driven by outside funding or delivered as a service to the community without laying the less visible foundations for transformational movement, the result is a counterfeit or simulated model. It looks good, but it won't multiply.

True models are essential to movements. Residents of model villages visualize what is possible and serve as magnets that draw people from villages throughout the surrounding area to see the transformation taking place. One model village can easily capture the attention of nine other villages, thus forming a *cluster* of ten. As other villages in the cluster are transformed, they too become models and magnets, and the movement expands. As development moves from village to village, guided by Christian facilitators, the gospel moves with it.

Multiplying into Village Clusters

Establishing a model village that has captured the attention of villages around it is the first step in catalyzing a transformational movement. The second step is a deliberate, intentional effort by the model village to multiply its successes into neighboring villages.

Even when you have a true model, a champion who is intentionally driving a plan is required to assure multiplication. That champion may come from the village itself or may be part of the training team that has been sent to the area to establish a model village and catalyze a movement. In theory, one would think this multiplication would be spontaneous. My experience, however, indicates that it is not.

In my travels, I have visited many "model" villages that were not multiplying. In most cases, either the five fundamentals of transformational ministry have been ignored, and the "model" is thus a counterfeit, or emerging leaders have not been envisioned and equipped by the trainers to facilitate multiplication into the cluster of villages around them. When the multiplication of trainers stops, the movement stalls out.

> The first step in catalyzing a transformational movement is a model village that has captured the attention of villages around. The second step is a deliberate, intentional effort by the model village to multiply its successes into neighboring villages.

Models are essential to movements, but there are often external forces, such as religion or politics, that are hostile to the spread of CHE and make movements extremely difficult, if not impossible, even where there is a model. In those situations, we are grateful for the opportunity just to serve in a single community.

I have witnessed multiplying movements in many different places, including Uganda, Zambia, Ethiopia, the Congo, India, Cambodia, Haiti, Central America, Central Asia, North Africa, China, the Philippines, and Papua New Guinea. Each of those situations included champions with a vision and passion to multiply and new trainers who were identified and equipped to facilitate the expansion. I have also observed that when the multiplication of trainers stops for any reason, the movement stalls out. The key to a growing movement is the training of trainers, or what we call TOT.

As part of our strategy for envisioning transformational movements, we are challenging ministries globally through million-village consultations in every country to adopt and target clusters of ten villages. We follow up by training and equipping their teams to establish a model village within the adopted cluster, and then we work intentionally to multiply the model into every village in the cluster.

> Our vision for catalyzing transformational movements in a million villages begins with ten thousand model villages multiplying into clusters of villages around them.

The first step in our vision to catalyze transformational movements in a million villages is to establish ten thousand strategically placed models that are multiplying the cluster of villages around them. At the end of that process, we envision one hundred thousand transformed communities, or ten thousand clusters of ten villages each.

Reaching a Tipping Point

Sociologists have observed that when 10 percent of a population is strongly advocating for a cause, a tipping point is reached, and the whole of the population will be impacted.[92] If we want a million-village movement, our tipping point is one hundred thousand. I have already explained in the previous section how we can get to one hundred thousand villages. I believe the church can be mobilized and equipped to strategically establish ten thousand model villages, and then intentionally multiply each of those models into one hundred thousand villages. If, by God's grace, we can achieve that, we will have reached our tipping point and launched a movement with the potential to impact a million villages. The following diagram illustrates the entire process.

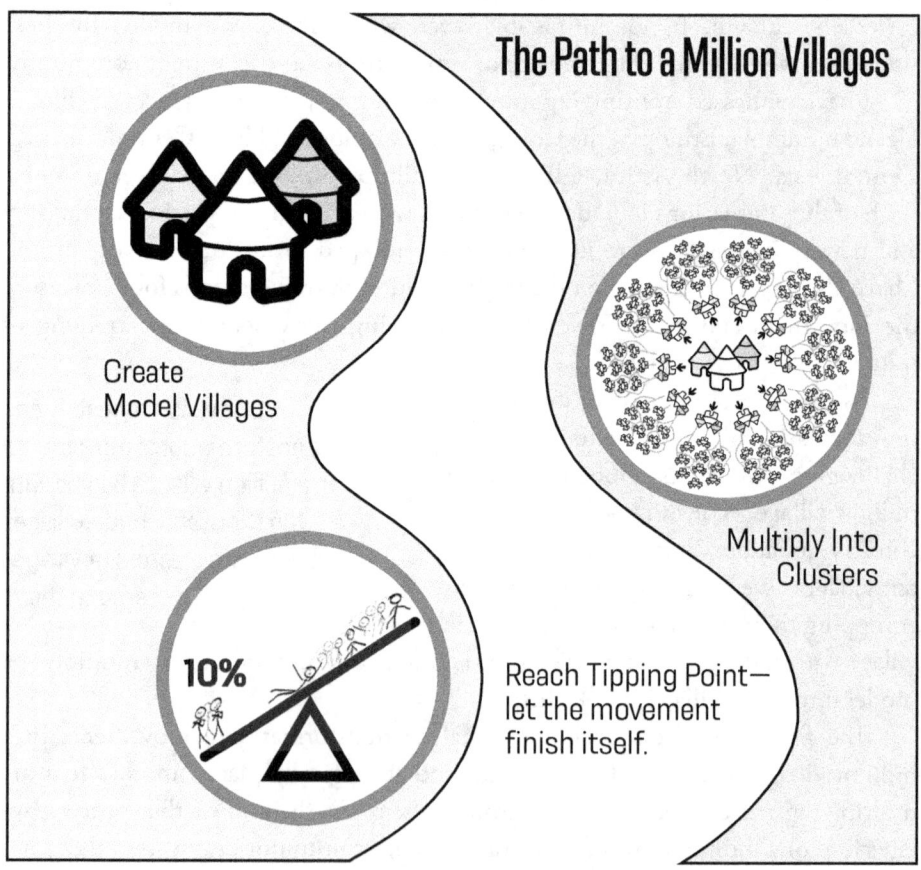

---

92 Malcolm Gladwell, *The Tipping Point: How Little Things Can Make a Big Difference* (Boston: Little, Brown & Co., 2006).

CHAPTER 9
Be Part of the Change

This final chapter represents an invitation for you to join the movement for change in a million villages. If you are seriously looking for a place to begin, then I want to suggest a path forward, offer some tools for catalyzing transformational movements in villages where you work, and help you get connected with others in the movement.

My transformational journey toward a more transformational ministry began with some basic commitments. It took me years to find my way—wrestling theologically with concepts of wholism and breaking free from the dualism that defined my life and work, seeking out a strategy and philosophy of ministry which brought evangelism and compassion together as an expression of obedience to everything that Jesus commanded, and finding like-minded colleagues who would walk forward with me. At the end of the road, I found I had made four big choices, commitments I would encourage you to consider as you seek your own path forward.

Four Commitments of a Change-Maker

In the next few paragraphs, I will describe the commitments God led me to make that changed the course of my entire ministry and produced a result far beyond what I could have ever hoped or imagined. I will then present some ideas for how you might take the same steps in your life.

The *first commitment* I made was to follow Jesus. I had no idea where he might take me, but I was willing to follow him. My heart's cry as a young believer was to know him and to follow in his footsteps wherever that might lead. Eventually that commitment led my wife and I and our young children to the Philippines as missionaries.

The *second commitment* I made, years later, was to bring evangelism and compassion together and to seek out a strategy that would effectively proclaim Christ in word and deed. I was compelled in my search by the conviction that I needed to quit prioritizing the commands of Christ and find a way to obey everything Jesus commanded. That led me to commit myself to wholistic ministry and eventually to use the strategy of CHE.

The *third commitment* I made was to the poor and marginalized. I listened as my Savior put himself in the place of the poor and said, "If you have done it to the least of these, you have done it to me." As a result, my commitment to the Lord Jesus required me to concern myself with the needs of the poor.

The *fourth commitment* I made was to work collaboratively with the body of Christ and to seek deliberately and intentionally to advance his kingdom rather than building my own. This was modeled for me by Stan Rowland, the founder of CHE and my mentor for more than twenty years. He insisted that whatever we have of value belongs to the kingdom and is to be shared. The greatest expression of that commitment was his refusal to copyright any of the CHE training material and his insistence on distributing it freely in a form that could be modified or translated for local use. The collection now includes almost ten thousand lessons on everything from agriculture and animal husbandry to disease prevention and spiritual growth.

These four commitments changed everything for me, producing results far beyond what I could have ever hoped or imagined in the lives of people all around the world. In the pages to follow, I will suggest some practical steps you might take to explore or follow through on each of these four commitments.

Commitment #1: Following Jesus

I am broken, and I live in a broken world. Evidence of this brokenness is all around me and within me. I look around me and I see broken families, poverty, oppression, injustice, violence, ghettos, illness, and death. I look within me and I see pride, envy, lust, prejudice, bitterness, greed, and laziness.

> **Change must begin from the inside. I need a new heart, and the world needs a Savior who can bring change from the inside out.**

I am condemned by my conscience because I know what I see within me falls short of what my own conscience tells me I should see: love, compassion, gentleness, humility, purity, integrity, peace, righteousness, justice, wisdom, and self-control. I understand from world history that something more than power and politics is needed to heal the brokenness I see within me and in the world around me. Change must begin from the inside. I need a new heart, and the world needs a Savior who can bring change from the inside out.

These observations, impressed on me by conscience, are affirmed in the teaching of the Scriptures. The story of the Bible is an accounting of the history of our brokenness and the pathway to our healing. The story begins with the revelation that we are not the product of random processes, but persons made in the image of God with the capacity to think, to appreciate, to choose, to relate, and to create. God made us in his image for fellowship with himself, and he put us on a planet which he designed for us to flourish.

Unfortunately, we chose to use the freedoms and capacities which God gave us to create a path toward destruction rather than toward the wholeness God intended for us. In the process we exalted ourselves above our Creator and moved in directions that he forbade. The results were catastrophic.

Theologians who study the Bible refer to the abandonment of God's designs and intentions by the first couple as "the fall." The story of the Bible is the revelation of God's plan to restore all that was broken by that fall.

The choice to abandon God's designs and intentions were initially made by the first couple in a place called the garden of Eden, but we all have participated in it. Our choices and behaviors flow from human hearts that are corrupt. Fellowship with God is broken; strife and shame have taken over our relationships; and the planet God created for our flourishing has been spoiled by suffering, pain, and death. In his grace, God allows this suffering. In fact, the Lord has imposed it because he wants us to see the error of our ways, repent of our corruption, and return to the life he intended. The Bible tells us that the answer to our brokenness is not the power and politics of corrupted hearts, but new hearts. We must repent and be born again.

In loving pursuit of his wayward children, God sent his Son Jesus to offer forgiveness of sin and the restoration of all things. This offering would be an incomprehensible display of unlimited love and profound mercy. By his life, Jesus taught us about and modeled for us the virtues of the path God intended. He called us to repentance, and he performed miracles demonstrating the desire and the power of God to heal the sick, raise the dead, feed the hungry, and calm the storm.

While teaching the virtues of the path God intended and demonstrating his power to restore all things, Jesus announced the kingdom of God had come near (Mark 1:15). He announced the purpose of his coming was to establish the rule and reign of God on the earth in ways that have never happened before in human history, and to usher in a new creation, perfect in righteousness and peace—a place in which all wrongs will be made right (Rev 21:1–5). Jesus went through every city and village, calling people to repentance and announcing the good news of the kingdom of God (Matt 4:23; 9:35; Mark 1:14–15; Luke 4:42; 8:1).

Sadly, Jesus was rejected by those to whom he offered the good news of the kingdom and eventually was handed over by the Jewish religious rulers of his day to be put to death by Roman crucifixion. The forces of evil claimed a momentary victory, seeming to have put to death all possibility of a return to the rule of God. But the battle was not over. Jesus rose from the dead, triumphing over sin and death, and has now been exalted to the right hand of the Father. By his death, Jesus carried our sin to the grave and bore its penalty, and by his resurrection he triumphed over death and every force of evil and inaugurated an eternal kingdom that will never again be shaken. He will return in the same way he ascended to heaven, execute judgment, and establish his reign in the new heaven and the new earth forever.

When you hear Jesus calling, he is offering you release from shame and the just penalty of sin and giving you a place in the new heaven and the new earth. He is also inviting you to participate with him in the restoration of all things—to be ambassadors of the kingdom of God. When you respond to his call, he saves you and then sends you to proclaim release from our brokenness and to bring the virtues and values of the coming kingdom into the present through your life and witness.

Commitment #2: Bringing Evangelism and Compassion Together

If my father's generation neglected social action in their fight against the social gospel, my son's generation will neglect evangelism in favor of social action. If we want to be faithful to the Scriptures and to the gospel Jesus preached, we must find and live in the radical middle where evangelism and compassion merge into ministries that proclaim salvation through faith in Christ while reflecting the values of the kingdom in the communities we serve.

The biggest hurdle in fulfilling my commitment to bring evangelism and compassion together was finding an effective strategy for doing it. I searched for a strategy that would address the root causes and release the world's poor from poverty with real solutions that change the trajectory of their lives forever. I also looked for a strategy that would bring evangelism and compassion together without using handouts and projects as mere inducements for conversion.

In my search, God brought me to Stan Rowland and to CHE. I found in CHE a proven strategy that seamlessly integrates evangelism, discipleship, and church planting with disease prevention and community-based development—a strategy that has been used effectively around the world to plant churches and lift communities out of cycles of poverty and disease. The CHE strategy and tools belong to the kingdom, not to any one ministry or organization. The curriculum isn't copyrighted, and those who are trained become trainers. CHE can be used by any organization or individual who wants to bring Christ to communities in word and deed. If you are interested in learning more, I invite you to sign up for the first phase of our training at a location in your area or region. See www.chenetwork.org.

Once you have completed the first phase of CHE training (TOT 1), you will be offered access to what I believe is the most extensive collection of lesson plans available anywhere for work in poor communities. The CHE curriculum includes lesson plans, manuals, pictures, and more—over fifteen thousand documents that can be used to facilitate learning in regard to almost any issue which rural communities face, empowering them to create real solutions that address the root causes of their poverty and are both sustainable and multipliable.

> If we want to be faithful to the gospel Jesus preached, we must merge evangelism and compassion into ministries that proclaim salvation through faith in Christ and reflect the values of the kingdom in the communities we serve.

Commitment #3: Change for the Poor

The third commitment I want to encourage you to consider—a commitment to the poor and marginalized—cannot be separated from the second—a commitment to bring evangelism and compassion together. Jesus put himself in the place of the poor and told his followers that service offered to the poor would be received as if it were offered to him. He went further to say he would separate the righteous from the unrighteous based upon how they treated the poor he represents (Matt 25:34–36, 40). Jesus identified himself as brother to the hungry, the thirsty, the stranger, the naked, the sick, and the prisoner. He calls us as his followers to do the same.

According to studies on multidimensional poverty published by the United Nations, 85 percent of the world's poor live in approximately one million rural villages. Many of these villages have no gospel witness among them. If we are serious about poverty alleviation and reaching the poor for Christ, then we must go to the village. We must intentionally find our way to some of the most remote places on earth, and we must not be content until the youngest girl in the darkest corner of the dreariest hut in the remotest village has hope.

> Jesus put himself in the place of the poor and told his followers that service offered to the poor would be received as if offered to him.

We are looking for champions and collaborating partners who share our passion. We invite you to receive CHE training and then join with hundreds of organizations working together in 136 countries to bring the gospel of the kingdom to the world's poorest.

Commitment #4: Collaboration

The fourth commitment I made, and am encouraging others to make, is to work together with others to do the big thing that none of us can do alone. I was captivated by a vision of what might be possible if I could be part of a global network with a proven strategy and the capacity to catalyze transformational movements that would change life for the poor in a million villages until Jesus returns.

Collaborating together broadens our perspectives, reduces duplication of effort, increases efficiency, and gives us access to innovations and best practices. It produces a combined action that is greater in total effect than the sum of our individual efforts. Collaboration gives us the power to do together what no one of us can do alone!

We live in a day when collaboration is not only possible but is the best practice. I am absolutely convinced that the next great frontier in mission is collaboration, and that anything less is arrogant.[93]

With information and connections at our fingertips through simple internet searches, barriers to collaboration can easily be overcome. Our next step is to make time to connect and set aside resources in our budgets to invest in collaborative efforts.

Just thirty years ago, when Jeannie and I went to the Philippines as missionaries, it took six weeks to connect with our family back home: three weeks for a letter we mailed to get across the ocean, and three more weeks for us to receive their reply. Phone calls were expensive and therefore were made only on special occasions. Flights were still relatively expensive, so we came home for deputation only once every four years. Connecting across the miles was difficult, denominational boundaries were strong, and missionaries often worked in silos. As a result, they were frequently unaware of what was going on, even nearby.

Together we can do the big thing that none of us can do alone.

This is not the situation today. With a quick search of the internet you can discover in an instant what ministries are nearby and who might be working on the same cause as you. Without leaving our desks, we can have online meetings with colleagues and partners from all over the world. Knowledge can be posted in one language and retrieved in another in seconds. We are the first generation in history to have access to such powerful tools that allow us to join hands and do together what no one of us can do alone.

Organizations with the foresight and discipline to invest in partnerships with others will lead the way in the future. Their ministries will be strengthened through the exchange of ideas, their causes will be advanced through shared resources, and they will make the big things possible that other ministries cannot do alone.

---

93 Geordon Rendle, president of Youth for Christ International, taken from a speech he delivered in France at the Transform World Leadership Summit in 2015.

There are reasons for resisting collaboration. Perhaps it matters too much who gets the credit, or we are unwilling to give up power and control. I am reminded, however, that the path to greatness in the kingdom is not power, but influence; not control, but service. True collaboration is void of power struggles, but instead calls us into the service of one another. Jesus put it this way: "Whoever wants to become great among you must be your servant, and whoever wants to be first must be your slave—just as the Son of Man did not come to be served, but to serve, and to give his life as a ransom for many" (Matt 20:26–28).

My commitment to collaboration led me establish the Global CHE Network in 2009. The Global CHE Network is an association of people and organizations working together in 136 countries (as of this writing), using the CHE strategy to catalyze transformational movements in a million villages. We are organizing into national coalitions, with a vision to bring new life to every village in every nation on earth.

The service team for the Global Network provides a large pool of resources from which all members can draw, including curriculum and digital resources. Conferences and internships provide opportunities for connection, continuing education, and mutual encouragement. National coalitions provide opportunity for members in a country to assemble annually and form partnerships for the transformation of the nation they serve.

To sign up for CHE training near you, go to www.chenetwork.org. Anyone who has completed the first phase of CHE training (TOT 1) can join the Global Network by applying online at www.chenetwork.org.

Tools and Connections for a Million-Village Movement

CHE Training

CHE Training of Trainers (TOT) is designed to equip participants to implement their own integrated ministry of community health and evangelism in a target area. The training is done in three phases. Each phase involves thirty-five hours of learning, followed by approximately six months in the field. CHE training is "just-in-time training," designed to give participants what they need to take the next step with their targeted communities.

The first phase of CHE training (TOT 1) is aimed at understanding the biblical basis for CHE and basic principles of wholistic community-based development. Participants learn steps for implementing CHE, how to choose a target community, and strategies for entering the community. Participants learn basic skills for raising awareness, organizing, and mobilizing the community for cooperative action through the formation of a development committee.

The second phase of CHE training (TOT 2) is designed to prepare trainers for two tasks: (1) equipping the development committee to lead the development process in their own community, and (2) training CHE volunteers for home visitation. TOT 2 focuses on capacity building for the committee, facilitation skills for the trainer, teaching methods and materials, and equipping the CHE volunteers.

The third phase of training (TOT 3) takes place after a CHE program is successfully adopted by a community. TOT 3 focuses on evaluation of the project as well as how to multiply the project into other areas. TOT 3 is training for multiplying change from village to village and catalyzing transformational movements. To sign up for CHE training near you, go to www.chenetwork.org.

CHE Curriculum

The CHE curriculum is a collection of best practices from around the world which are condensed into simple participatory lesson plans that can be taught in the community. Lesson plans are made available as Microsoft Word documents so that they can easily be adapted to the context by the end users. The latest set of CHE materials contains more than ten thousand documents, including lesson plans, stories, picture books, teaching aids, surveys, and tools for monitoring and evaluation. This material is available in the member area of the website.

CHE Collaboration

The Global CHE Network is an association of people and organizations around the world who are using the CHE strategy. The goal of our collaboration is the strengthening of each individual ministry and the expansion of CHE ministries as a whole. We are networked together for mutual support to share useful ideas and best practices, encourage one another, coordinate efforts, and optimize the use of limited resources.

The network provides a large pool of resources from which all members can draw. By coordinating our efforts with a determination to build up all member ministries and expand the CHE movement, we gain access to ideas and resources. Members train individuals and organizations in their sphere of influence for effective wholistic ministry, thus widening the circle from which to find encouragement, share resources, and plan strategically for the greatest possible impact.

Coordinators are identified by various members to facilitate working groups that bring everyone doing CHE in a country or region together for fellowship, encouragement, planning, and exchanging ideas. Members of the network also host CHE internships annually in the Philippines, Guatemala, Ghana, Kenya, and other nations, in order to equip these coordinators as catalysts and mentors in their country, people group, or other sphere of influence. In this way we create new opportunities to do together what none of us could achieve alone. For more information about the network, go to www.chenetwork.org.

Conclusion

Join the movement and embrace the opportunity to work together with others around the world to bring the love and truth of the good news to a million villages.

We face an opportunity today that has not existed since the beginning of church history—the opportunity to accelerate the advance of the gospel to the farthest reaches of our world with the love and truth of that good news. In order to achieve this million-village vision, we will need to move beyond projects to transformational movements—BEYOND POVERTY.

My goal for this book is to lay out the biblical basis for wholistic ministry and the foundational principles for transformational movements. I have shared inspiring stories about movements that have been started by ordinary people with a passion to be obedient to the cause of Christ. Hopefully you have been able, in the process, to envision a role for yourself in the call to bring new life to a million villages.

Appendix A

What Others Are Saying About CHE

CHE is by far the most effective method of wholistic discipleship I have ever seen.
            Dennis Wadley, CEO, Liebenzell USA

Once our team received CHE training, we immediately adopted it as our primary strategy. It has been the single most successful "life changer" for the community.
            Jason Law, Founder/CEO, 1MISSION

CHE brings together Jesus' Great Commission and Greatest Commandments. If we apply these principles effectively, CHE will transform the way we do missions. In fact, the transformation has already begun.
            Doug Lucas, Founder and President, Team Expansion

CHE is a powerful and effective strategy for community mobilization. Its power is not based on material resources; it is based on knowledge transfer and personal and spiritual empowerment.
            Dr. Milton B. Amayun and **Dr. Alan Talens**
            Evaluation report, Philippines

In over twenty years of two-thirds world ministry, having evaluated dozens of wholistic programs in numerous countries, we have not seen anywhere such dramatic impact for such little cost.
            Dr. James F. Engle, **Dr. Terry Andrews**, and **Dr. Sam Voorhies**
            Evaluation report, Congo

Appendix B

A Brief History of Community Health Evangelism

I want to give tribute to a champion of wholistic ministry. He wasn't part of the elite discussions at Lausanne about the relationship between social action and evangelism, but after Lausanne he went to work in the trenches, figuring out how to do wholistic ministry in meaningful ways. In my estimation, he has done as much to promote wholistic mission in the evangelical church as anyone. After the Lausanne Conference and before the convening of the Grand Rapids gathering, Bill Bright, founder of Campus Crusade for Christ (now Cru), asked businessman Stan Rowland to draft a proposal for a ministry that would integrate curative care, health education, community development, and spiritual growth. This document, drafted in 1978, was the beginning of the development of the CHE strategy.

In the decades to come, Stan's work and the ministry model he created would span the globe, touching the lives of villagers all over the world and sparking the imagination of the church at every turn. Key core values that have been operative within CHE from the beginning include *transferability* from one to another, the power of *multiplication*, and *integration of word and deed* into one seamless whole.

The first CHE project, which was clinic-based, was initiated in Keriocho, Uganda, in 1980. Due to the proximity of the fighting in the Ugandan civil war (1981–86), the clinic closed in 1982 and the team moved to Buhugu, Uganda. About that same time, three more projects were initiated in Uganda and two in Kenya. These programs were largely agricultural and community-based. The key to ministry during those years was to develop a model that could meet the core values previously mentioned.

Stan moved to the Nairobi Campus Crusade office in 1986, and thus CHE programs were initiated in East Africa. CHE workers used a participatory style of teaching that enabled learners to create their own solutions and encouraged self-discovery. This learning process allowed for discovery to turn into action under the guidance of the Holy Spirit. And since the lesson plans facilitated and enabled transferability, other English-speaking African countries soon started to develop CHE programs.

The first Training of Trainers (TOT) was held in 1986 for Cru and other agencies. This further enhanced the spread and multiplication of CHE. Programs became community owned rather than organization driven, and preventive rather than curative in structure. Putting into practice what had been learned from the initial development in Uganda, over one hundred teams from more than forty ministries were trained in CHE in Uganda, Kenya, Tanzania, South Africa, and Swaziland between 1986 and 1990.

In 1989, CHE began to be used by Medical Ambassadors International (MAI), even as Cru was phasing out the Agape Movement of which CHE was a part. The concept of the CHE strategy introduced a new paradigm for MAI, which up to that time had been focused on curative clinics and spiritual ministry. All curative programs in the Philippines and Guatemala were immediately converted to focusing on development and disease prevention. From there, CHE spread to Central America and then to Bangladesh, India, Central Asia, and China, using a restricted access model. Most of these new sites were under MAI leadership.

In 1990, Stan moved his work with CHE from Campus Crusade for Christ to Medical Ambassadors International (MAI), which at that time was under the leadership of president and CEO, Dr. Paul Calhoun. CHE would go on to become MAI's sole method of ministry.

Medical Ambassadors raised up field workers to multiply CHE worldwide. I became one of those workers. We held TOTs to bring training and coaching to other agencies, visiting their programs and working under cooperative agreements. By 2000, CHE had spread from nine to forty-two countries and was working with several hundred mission agencies, churches, and denominations globally.

The MAI field leadership was committed to using CHE to facilitate a movement of integrated ministry to the poor. The challenge was to transform CHE from a ministry that was driven and controlled by a single organization into a tool owned by all who used it. So in 2003 MAI changed its leadership structure to an inverted pyramid to facilitate an increasingly servant-like style of leadership. The title "field director" was changed to "field coordinator." Less control from headquarters meant more control in the field. The first regional council, bringing together leaders from all over Southeast Asia, proved a successful early step in moving ownership of CHE from MAI to the field. Soon regional and area councils were coming together all around the world.

By 2006, CHE had spread to seventy-two countries with programs on five continents and in all major religious and political blocks. In order to deal with the risk of dilution and weakening of the CHE strategy due to its ever-widening influence, participating agencies were asked to agree to CHE's core values.

The use of the CHE strategy was mushrooming, yet the goal of shared ownership was elusive. CHE still had the appearance of being driven by MAI, even though the focus was no longer on programs funded by the organization but on the entire network of agencies using CHE.

A Brief History of the Global CHE Network

As leaders at MAI, we saw our impact expand exponentially as the work of people and organizations we trained and mentored flourished. Again and again we watched as our partners from different cultures and in varying religious and political contexts used the CHE strategy to bring people to faith in Christ, plant churches, and alleviate poverty. We developed a profound conviction that CHE was very useful to the church for outreach to the poor, and that it was incumbent on us to share it. The strategy didn't belong to us, but to the kingdom.

In 2005, an appraisal of the impact of our work worldwide revealed that those we were training were seeing the same kind of results we were. In fact, some of our partners' programs outperformed our own! By the end of 2005, only 81 of the 312 known CHE programs worldwide were funded by MAI. That meant 74 percent of our impact wasn't coming from the projects we managed but from sharing what we had been given with others. This led us to the conviction that while there was value in managing our own programs, our greatest impact would come from training and equipping others. We sensed God was calling us not just to manage programs, but to launch transformational movements.

The next steps toward continuing expansion would take a lot from us and test our resolve:

- We had to demonstrate by our actions that we placed kingdom values ahead of the preservation and growth of our own organization.
- We had to value the cause more than the power.
- We had to step down as owners of the strategy and allow it to be owned by others.
- We had to continue the distribution of our CHE curriculum without copyright[94] and allow others to modify the material for use in their context.
- We had to give up our "territories" and value collaboration over control.
- We had to rethink our roles and learn new skills, learning to make movements rather than manage programs.[95]
- We had to set up an association that would allow users to be able to come to the table as owners rather than stand aside as consumers.

---

94 The open source CHE curriculum now contains more than ten thousand lesson plans on a whole range of development topics.

95 Managers of successful CHE programs learned to be consultants first, and then network facilitators. They equipped other ministries for CHE work, and then brought the CHE practitioners from different organizations in a country or region together to form working groups or counsels. This was the beginning of what would emerge as the Global CHE Network.

- We had to learn to facilitate collaboration rather than give direction and to make it our goal to strengthen other ministries as well as our own.
- We had to invest in others and commit both funding and personnel to the establishment of the Global CHE Network. Every one of these changes was extremely challenging and demanded much more of us than we imagined.

By 2008, we as leaders at MAI had come to the conviction that a new structure would be required if the CHE movement was to continue to expand and reach its full potential. We would need to allow the CHE movement to increase beyond the control of our own purview and allow other organizations to take ownership of the strategy and the movement. In response, we set up an association called the Global CHE Network and took our place as a member of the association rather than the center of the CHE world.[96]

The establishment of an association required significant operational as well as structural changes. In order to bring about a large networking organization such as GCN, several radical changes in thought and operation had to take place. Among the most significant, I would step down as international coordinator at MAI to found and coordinate the formation of the network. Production and distribution of CHE curriculum would be handed over to and shared with the network. The network would have to establish systems for communication and decision-making between organizations and become financially independent, finding sustainable ways to generate income.

Even after making these changes, enormous obstacles remained. Many churches and mission agencies are consumed by internal goals and objectives and therefore have no room in their budgets or time in their schedules that would allow their associates to fully participate in network activities like this. The leadership of the network would have to overcome these hurdles and find a way to communicate the value and benefit of working together to achieve a greater end. We would have to build a shared vision of what we can do together that goes beyond what we can achieve alone. We would have to have a set of core values that would bind us together and shape our common efforts.[97]

At a more basic level, if the movement was to reach its full potential, we would be required to articulate the wholistic nature of the gospel and facilitate a shift in the thinking of many evangelicals about the very definition

---

96 The Global CHE Network is an association of people and organizations using the strategy of Community Health Evangelism to serve impoverished communities in urban slums and rural poor communities around the world. We are networked together for mutual support to share useful ideas and best practices, encourage each other, coordinate efforts, and optimize the use of limited resources.

97 CHE's core values are integration and wholism, commitment to the poor and marginalized, developmental approaches that break the cycle of poverty and disease, local ownership and initiative, multiplication and movements, Christian servant leadership, and contextualization.

of Christian mission. We would become champions of the idea that as followers of Christ we aren't called just to save souls, but to make followers of Jesus, organized in local fellowships which reflect the fullness of the kingdom of God in their communities by complete obedience to everything Jesus commanded.

Championing this message wouldn't be easy, because it is a call to change. The wholisitc message of the gospel of the kingdom challenges assumptions and deeply entrenched traditions, thus calling for major shifts in the preferred methods and strategies of many churches and parachurch organizations.

The network was formed in 2009, as core values were established and associational structures and leadership were put in place. As of this writing, network members have ministries in 136 countries, representing more than 960 denominations or faith-based organizations. Individual ministries are being strengthened, and the movement is growing.

CHE for Urban Neighborhoods: Neighborhood Transformation (NT)

In 2005, Stan Rowland began to develop a CHE model for work in urban America. Neighborhood Transformation (NT) is a strategy to help churches minister wholistically to people living in urban, poor neighborhoods. NT seeks to connect neighbors, create community, and transform neighborhoods. Using an asset-based approach, this modified strategy empowers people to move away from unhealthy dependencies toward freedom and self-reliance.

After NT found its first application in the greater Phoenix area, Stan founded the Collaborative for Neighborhood Transformation (www.neighborhoodtransformation.net) in 2009. His desire was to expand this urban CHE model to cities throughout North America and around the world. As with the Global CHE Network, members and partnering organizations mutually encourage, motivate, and innovate on behalf of under-served communities. Today, several other cities across the United States have implemented NT and are seeing the kind of transformation that only comes from a Christ-centered model.

Bibliography

Ajulu, D. 1996. *Holism in Development.* Monrovia, CA: MARC.

Amayun, M. B., and A. Talens. 2001. "Community Health Evangelism: Health and Holism for the Philippines' Rural Poor: An Evaluation Report on Medical Ambassadors' Program in Antique and Surigao, the Philippines." Spring Lake, MI: Rushing Wind Foundation. Medical Ambassadors International: 225.

Chambers, R. 1993. *Challenging the Professions: Frontiers for Rural Development.* London: IT Pubs.

Crocker, D. A. 1991. "Toward Development Ethics." *World Development* 19, no. 5: 457–83.

Donovan, V. 1978. *Christianity Rediscovered.* Maryknoll, NY: Orbis Publications.

Drabek, A. G. 1987. "Development Alternatives: The Challenge for NGOs." *World Development* 15 Supplement.

Elmer, D., and L. McKinney, eds. 1996. *With an Eye on the Future: Development and Mission in the 21st Century.* Monrovia, CA: MARC.

Engel, J. F. 2002. "Impact Evaluation: Community Health Evangelism Project, The Democratic Republic of the Congo": 61.

Engel, J. F., and W. A. Dyrness. 2000. *Changing the Mind of Missions.* Downers Grove, IL: InterVarsity.

Feuillerat, B. 2003. "AOG Mid Term Review Survey Report: Community Health Education Program, Assemblies of God—Cambodia."

Food for the Hungry International. 2004. "FHI Annual Evaluation Guidelines."

France, R. T. 1986. "Liberation in the New Testament." *Transformation* (January): 3–23.

Friere, P. 2003. *Pedagogy of the Oppressed.* New York: The Continuum International Publishing Group.

Gallup, George H. 1992. *The Saints Among Us.* Ridgefield, CT: Morehouse Pub Co.

Goulet, D. 1983. "Obstacles to World Development: An Ethical Reflection." *World Development* 2, no. 7: 609–24.

Gran, G. 1983. *Development by People: Citizen Construction of a Just World.* New York: Praeger.

Gustafson, J. W. 1998. "The Integration of Development and Evangelism." *Missiology: An International Review* 26, no. 2: 131–42.

Hawtrey, K. 1990. "The Oxford Declaration on Christian Faith and Economics." *Transformation* 7, no. 2.

Horstia, E., and P. Lal. 2003. "Mid-term Review of the Community Health Education (CHE) Programme in Cambodia." Review Report, CoPlan Consulting, Fida International.

James, Glenn, Elda Martinez, and Sherry Herbers, "What Can Jesus Teach Us about Student Engagement?" *Journal of Catholic Education* (September 2015).

Medical Ambassadors. 2005. "Internal Monitoring and Report Summaries." CHE Report, Modesto, CA.

Medical Ambassadors International. 2004. "MAI's Vision, Mission and Values."

Miller, D. 1998. *Discipling the Nations*. Seattle: YWAM.

Morgan, P. 1983. "The Project Orthodoxy in Development: Re-evaluating the Cutting Edge." *Public Administration and Development* 3: 329–39.

Nolan, C. 1994. "For Love and for Money, the Impact of Paying Volunteers in One Branch of a Volunteer-Led Agency." London School of Economics: 31.

Nyerere, J. 1976. "Declaration of Dar es Salaam." *Convergence* no. 4: 9–16.

Rondinelli, D. A. 1983. *Development Projects as Policy Experiments: An Adaptive Approach to Development Administration*. London: Methuen.

Rowland, S. 2001. *Multiplying Light and Truth through Community Health Evangelism*. Mumbai, India: GLS Publishing.

Rowland, S. 2002. "CHE Core Values." Medical Ambassadors International.

Rowland, S. 2003. "CHE Overview." Medical Ambassadors International.

Samuel, V., and C. Sugden, eds. 1999. *Mission as Transformation*. Oxford: Regnum.

Semoja, J., and O. Therkildsen, eds. 1995. "Service Provision under Stress in East Africa: Bringing Volunteerism Back In." Copenhagen, Centre for Development Research.

Shepherd, A. 1998. *Sustainable Rural Development*. New York: St. Martin's Press.

Shoo, R. 2003. "Primary Health Care Ambassadors Foundation Mid-term Evaluation Report," World Vision Tanzania, Consultancy Services Unit: 77.

Sider, R. 1981. *Evangelicals and Development*. Exeter, UK: Paternoster Press.

Sider, R. 1993. *Evangelism and Social Action*. London: Hodder and Stoughton.

Stott, J. R. 1975. *Christian Mission in the Modern World*. London: Falcon.

Sugden, C. 2000. *Gospel, Culture and Transformation*. Oxford: Regnum.

Wallance, R., S. Crowther, et al. 1997. *The Standardisation of Development: Influences on UK NGOs, Policies and Procedures*. Oxford: Worldview Press.

World Vision Development Resources Team. 2002. "Transformational Development Indicators." Washington DC.

Yamamore, T., B. Myers, et al., eds. 1995. *Serving with the Poor in Asia*. Monrovia, CA: MARC.

About the Author

Terry Dalrymple

Mobilizing and equipping workers for transformational community development among the poorest of the poor.

For twenty-seven years, Terry has championed the cause of the multidimensionally poor, training and mobilizing workers for transformational community development using a strategy called Community Health Evangelism (CHE). After a decade of service in the Philippines, Terry pioneered for Medical Ambassadors International in 9 countries in Southeast Asia, working together with partners to establish CHE programs in more than 400 communities. Later as International Coordinator at Medical Ambassadors, he guided the expansion of a growing global movement.

In 2009, Terry founded the Global CHE Network (CHE), an alliance of organizations in 115 countries working together to bring wholistic transformation to a million villages.

Additional Resources @ missionbooks.org

Village Medical Manual (7th ed.)
A Guide to Health Care in Developing Countries
Mary Vandekooi, M.D., D.T.M. & H.

Village Medical Manual is a user-friendly, two-volume healthcare guide for lay workers in developing countries with special features that trained medical professionals would also find useful.

Its intended use is for those who are required, by location and circumstances, to render medical care.

The clear vocabulary, along with over a thousand illustrations and diagrams, help Western-educated expatriates living in isolated locations to medically treat people and intelligently refer those that can be referred accordingly. It contains clearly defined procedural techniques and diagnostic protocols for when sophisticated instrumentation and lab tests are not available. It also offers solutions and advice for overcoming barriers to best practices in global health.

Volume 1 elucidates medical principles, symptoms, and procedures for routine medical care, as well as emergency situations.

Volume 2 includes vast symptom, disease (common and tropical), drug, and regionally-relevant indices to assist the reader in step-by-step diagnoses and treatment.

Now available in combined two-volume ebook @ Apple Books.

Health for All: The Vanga Story
Daniel Fountain

When Dan Fountain and his wife arrived in the Congo in 1961, the challenges to effective medical missions seemed overwhelming. As the only doctor for a quarter of a million residents of the Vanga Health Zone, and with nothing but a dilapidated mission hospital and an undertrained staff to run it, Dr. Fountain turned to prayer, innovation, and local partnerships to meet the vast needs of his area.

Health for All tells the story of an ever-increasing vision—from curative care to community health, from a barely functioning hospital to a network of successful health services, from a lack of qualified workers to a local residency training program, from biomedical reductionism to whole person care, from cultural stalemate to worldview transformation. Dr. Fountain's insights into health and wholeness have changed countless lives and communities. Part memoir, part history, part textbook, *Health for All* is the legacy of a man who patterned his life and labor after that of the Great Physician.

Additional Resources @ missionbooks.org

Empowering Children
Ravi Jayakaran

Empowering Children is especially designed for field practitioners seeking ways to encourage young people—particularly the marginalized—to become more involved in changing their circumstances. Through dozens of exercises and lessons, the book presents a variety of practical methods for engaging children in the development process—from assessments to evaluations. Discussions on issues such as personal empowerment, self-esteem, problem analysis, and child protection can equip leaders to help children serve as agents of change who understand how valuable they are. The book concludes with preparations for a community child participation plan. From a Christian perspective, the realization that all children have dignity and are created in the image of God helps us to see that every child's input is valuable. The Bible's concepts of community, church, and mission further help us to see that God not only uses kids in his wonderful plan, but that he also wants all of his children—male, female, young, and old—to participate in his work in the world.

Health, Healing and Shalom: Frontiers and Challenges for Christian Healthcare Missions
Bryant L. Myers, Erin Dufault-Hunter, Isaac B. Voss, editors

Ever since Jesus's proclamation in word and deed as the Great Physician, his followers in mission have assumed that salvation and health are intertwined. Yet for every age, Christians need to examine how they can best announce the gospel message of God's healing in word and deed in their own context. In our era, we are often simultaneously grateful for modern medicine and frustrated by its inability to care for the whole person in effective, affordable ways.

In this edited volume, authors with an interest in health missions from a wide variety of experiences and disciplines examine health and healing through the theological lens of shalom. This word, often translated "peace," names a much more complex understanding of human well-being as right relationships with one another, with God, and with creation. Reading various aspects of healthcare missions through these glasses not only yields much-needed correctives to current practice but also exposes the Spirit's invitation to participate in God's ongoing work of tending, caring, and healing our broken world.